# SiNGAPORE
# SHOPHOUSE

# SINGAPORE
# SHOPHOUSE

Text
Julian Davison

Photography
Luca Invernizzi Tettoni

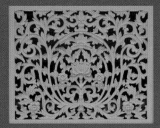

**Publisher**

© 2010, 2015 Talisman Publishing Pte Ltd

52 Genting Lane #06-05 Ruby Land Complex 1

Singapore 349560

**Text** © Julian Davison

**Photography** © Luca Invernizzi Tettoni

**Editor** Kim Inglis

**Designer** Norreha Sayuti

All rights reserved. No part of this book may be reproduced in any form or by any means without permission in writing from the publisher, except by a reviewer who may quote brief passages in a review.

Printed in Singapore

ISBN 978-981-05-9716-0

**Page 2**  Leafy five-foot-way on Duxton Hill.

**Pages 3–4**  Beautifully preserved terrace row on Everitt Road, Katong.

**Overleaf**  Front porch, the Baba House, Neil Road.

**Pages 9–10**  Asian-inspired front room of a Spottiswoode Park Road shophouse.

NATIONAL
ARCHIVES
OF SINGAPORE

# DEFINING THE SHOPHOUSE

**1**

# 2

# DEVELOPMENT OF THE SHOPHOUSE

# 3

# THE SHOPHOUSE TODAY

# DEFINING
# THE
# SHOPHOUSE

1

# DEFINING THE SHOPHOUSE

The archetypal Singapore shophouse is a two- or three-storey building with shop premises on the ground floor and living accommodation above. The ground floor is set back a little from the road while the upper storey, supported by a brace of columns, projects forward in line with the edge of the street to create a covered verandah in front of the shop. Shophouses were always conceived as being combined to form a terrace — a row of similar units built side by side with shared party walls making up one side of a street or city block. This being the case, the front verandah of every shophouse at street level is contiguous with its neighbour on either side, effectively creating a continuous covered walkway or colonnade in front of the shops along which passers-by may stroll, protected from both the sun and the rain.

Traditionally, the shophouse was built as the home of a merchant and his family. Business was conducted from the front room on the ground floor while the family occupied the rear of the building and the rooms on the floors above. However, as Singapore developed and became home to huge numbers of Chinese immigrants, many of the richer families moved out of the centre of town into "dwelling houses". More or less identical to shophouses in terms of layout and internal organisation, the major difference was that the front room on the ground floor was the principal reception room for receiving guests and visitors, rather than a space used for doing business.

ABOVE  Plaques stylised as Chinese scrolls, depicting morally uplifting scenes, were often placed over doors and windows.

OPPOSITE  This highly ornamented corner shophouse on Balestier Road encapsulates the quintessence of the Singapore shophouse, with its eclectic mix of Western and Chinese elements. Built in 1927 it exemplifies the popular Chinoiserie style of the late 1920s, with its richly ornamented surfaces and traditional Chinese plant and animal iconography.

# A LONG AND NARROW PLAN

The street frontage of a traditional shophouse was quite narrow — as wide as could be spanned feasibly by a single timber beam in the days before reinforced concrete — but the buildings often extended backwards from the street a fair way. The typical frontage was between 16 to 18 feet (6 m), with an average depth of around 80 feet (25 m), although some of the older houses could extend back twice as far. This characteristic ground plan has its origins in ancient China where house taxes were calculated according to a building's width or frontage on to the street. The Dutch in Malacca adopted a similar system of taxation, as did the East India Company in Penang; by the time members of Raffles' Land Allotment Committee came to drawing up a town plan for the future development of Singapore in 1822, it seemed only natural to them to parcel the land into shophouse-size building plots, some 20 feet (7 m) across.

The earliest shophouses in Singapore were pretty rudimentary: just one room deep, two storeys in height, with a pitched

roof on top, the ridgepole running parallel to the street. Each shophouse unit shared a party wall with its neighbours, the roof being supported by purlins running between the party walls. The latter extended above the roof ridge by around 18 inches (50 cm) to create a "fire wall", reducing the risk of fire spreading from one unit to another. The interior was lit by airwells, or narrow courtyards, open to the sky, which helped with ventilation and cooling of the building. An enclosed yard at the back was used for meal preparation on a brick-built, charcoal-burning hearth, with a roof over it to keep off the rain. This is also where clothes were laundered and the occupants of the house bathed, with water drawn from a well. The privy was situated here too.

The shophouse, then, in its most basic form, was clearly a fairly modest affair, but it was one that could easily be added to, simply by erecting a second building at the rear of the site, so that what was originally the backyard now became an internal courtyard, or airwell, separating the two built structures, with the cooking arrangements and so forth being transferred to the rear of the new construction. The process could be repeated a second, and even a third time, depending on how far back the site extended. In southern China, in the coastal regions of Guangdong province, from where many of Singapore's early immigrants hailed, this kind of dwelling is referred as a "bamboo house" (*zhugangcuo*), not because it was built of bamboo, but because of the linear nature of its layout where rooms and courtyards are arranged sequentially like the nodular sections of a bamboo culm. There are some instances of shophouses in Singapore with three or more airwells and a depth of more than 200 feet (approximately 60 m), although the great majority were less than half that length.

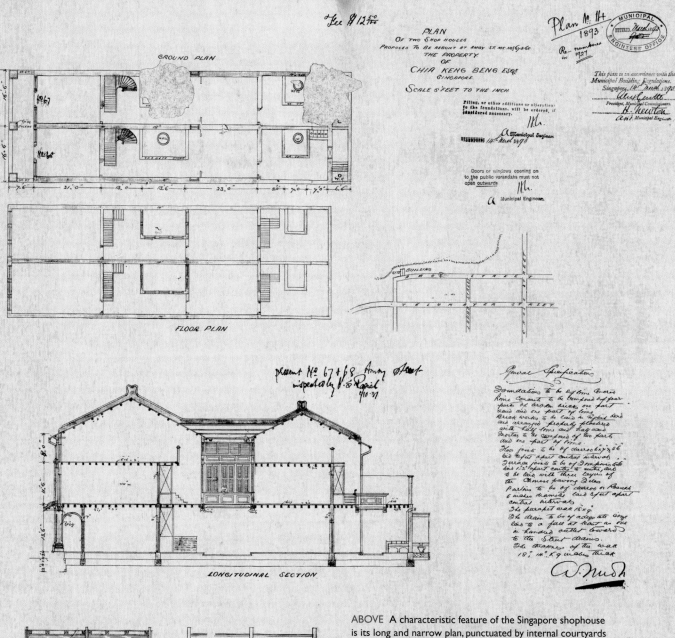

GROUND PLAN

FLOOR PLAN

PLAN
OF TWO SHOP HOUSES
PROPOSED TO BE REBUILT AT AMOY ST. NC. No367&368
THE PROPERTY
OF
CHIA KENG BENG ESQ.
SINGAPORE
SCALE 8 FEET TO THE INCH.

LONGITUDINAL SECTION

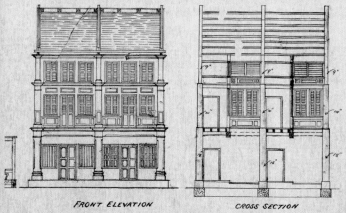

FRONT ELEVATION

CROSS SECTION

**ABOVE** A characteristic feature of the Singapore shophouse
is its long and narrow plan, punctuated by internal courtyards
or airwells that bring light and ventilation to the centre of the
building. The basic concept originated in Mainland Chinese
architecture, and was introduced to the region by Chinese
merchants — similar buildings can be found in Malacca and other
ancient city ports along the shores of maritime South East Asia.

In the 19th century, before the introduction of a piped water
supply, most shophouses had their own well, as shown here,
though the water drawn from it was often far from potable.

These working drawings date from 1893 and come from
the drawing board of a gentleman by the name of Wee Teck
Moh who was one of Singapore's most prolific shophouse
architects at the turn of the last century. One of the two units
depicted is still standing in Amoy Street, next door to the Siang
Cho Keong Temple (opposite).

# THE IMPORTANCE OF SYMMETRY

As in so many Asian architectural traditions, a correct orientation in relation to the environment and the proper alignment of built structures, in a ritual sense, are of the utmost importance in Chinese architecture. The shophouse form is ultimately based on the traditional Chinese courtyard house, which ideally was symmetrically planned along a north-south axis, with the most important or prestigious structure — the main hall or *zhengwu* — being at the north end and facing south. Subsidiary buildings were then placed to the left and right, with the main entrance completing the southern end of the compound, thereby creating an enclosed courtyard at the centre of the site.

The north-south alignment was a climatic adaptation to the rigours of winter in China's more northerly climes, but it also had ritual connotations deriving from the Chinese view of the universe as an integrated whole in which every aspect of the natural world is interrelated in a hugely complex system of opposing and complementary forces. In the traditional scheme of things, the main hall, while it is situated at the northern end of the compound, which is associated with winter, faces south which is propitious, being identified with the warm summer months, from which numerous other positive connotations can be drawn. This is where the shrine dedicated to family's ancestors is situated, the cultivation of respectful and propitious relations with one's deceased forebears being one of the central tenets of Chinese religion.

When it came to shophouses, the north-south axis was subjugated by the dictates of pre-existing street plans and urban topographies, though a north-south orientation was still regarded favourably, especially since, in the case of the Singapore shophouse it reduced the effect of solar radiation. More importantly, the layout of the shophouse, and the particular significance that was attached to individual rooms, in principle remained the same, regardless of whether or not the building was aligned on a true north-south axis. Thus, the front room on the ground floor — whether it was used as a reception room for receiving visitors or

190428 (Tallman)

for commercial purposes — was equated with the southern pavilion in a courtyard house where guests were traditionally received and entertained. Similarly, the room housing the shrine dedicated to the family's ancestors was situated at the rear of the shophouse, with the airwell in between, a position that corresponds to the situation of the ancestral hall at the northern end of the compound facing south across the courtyard.

As far as symmetry is concerned, since a shophouse was seldom more than one room in width, there was not much scope for its expression in terms of the ground plan. Where we do see it, however, is it in the organisation of the façade — the symmetrical arrangement of doors and windows about a central axis — and the internal placement of the furnishings — the central location of altars, the balanced arrangement of furniture in the front reception room of townhouses, and the symmetrical positioning of internal doors, leading from one room to another.

OPPOSITE  The concept of symmetry is one of the most fundamental axioms in Chinese architecture, just as it is in the Western Classical tradition, and we see this correspondence perfectly demonstrated in this late-19th century shophouse in Telok Ayer Street, which combines both Chinese and European architectural elements in a successful meeting of East and West.

ABOVE  A traditional Chinese courtyard house, or *siheyuan* (literally 'four-sided yard'), based on Taiwanese sources. The ancestral hall is situated on the far side of the courtyard, facing the reception hall and entrance to the compound at the southern end of the site, with the rest of the buildings symmetrically arranged on either side. The *siheyuan* was the home of choice for the wealthy Chinese merchant or gentlemen of independent means, and it was an ideal that Chinese took with them wherever they went: at least half a dozen courtyard houses are known to have been built in Singapore, though only the home of Towkay Tan Yeok Nee has survived intact to this day (see pages 94–97).

# BRICKS AND MORTAR

In terms of their construction, shophouses were built of locally manufactured bricks, brick-making being one of the first industries to be

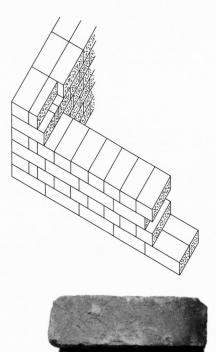

established in Singapore after the island was settled by the British in 1819. Bricks were made by hand according to the slop moulding method where the brick is formed in a rectangular mould with no bottom or top. The mould is first wetted and placed on the ground and then filled with a very wet clay mixture. Excess clay is scraped off with a trowel and the top smoothed over. The mould is then lifted off and the brick left on the ground to dry. Finally, the brick is fired in a kiln.

Needless to say, this was a very labour intensive method, but contemporary accounts record that a team of four — one man to mould the bricks, a second to supply him with clay, and two more to remove the moulds — could average three bricks a minute. In the early days of the Settlement, the quality was also very variable, but this improved after 1844 when the Public Works Department set up its own kiln along Serangoon Road supervised by a trained brick maker from England.

Piles, which were often necessary in Singapore's uncertain soils, comprised staves of rot-resistant *bakau* (mangrove) wood driven vertically into the ground; sometimes short lengths of *balau* wood, laid crossways and lengthwise, were used instead. The foundations consisted of masonry rubble set in lime mortar. The latter was produced locally, and comprised one part lime to two parts sand, the best sand being the fine-grained alluvial sort found in local rivers, while the lime (calcium oxide) was produced from burnt coral or marine shells. As far as the masonry walls were concerned, architects' specifications often stipulated that the bricks should be laid in English bond (see left), using "good-quality lime mortar", mixed to the same specifications as above.

TOP  There are numerous ways in which a brick wall can be laid; the illustration shows the "English bond" method, where bricks are placed transversely and then longitudinally, in alternating bands. This is recognised as a particularly strong bonding technique for brick walls and was frequently specified in 19th century working drawings. Above we see a 19th-century hand made brick.

OPPOSITE  Walls were rendered in a plaster made from river sand and lime, usually mixed in equal proportions. They were then given a coat of lime wash, creamy white, yellow ochre and especially indigo being the most popular colours during the early period. The latter was made from *Indigo tinctoria*, which was imported from India where it was produced in huge quantities in the 19th century. This surface was semi-permeable allowing moisture to rise from the base of the walls and evaporate which had a cooling effect. Note the use of English bond (bottom left).

# THE FIVE-FOOT WAY

The front porch or verandah, open at either end, is a quintessential feature of shophouse architecture. Referred to as a "five-foot way" because this was the minimum width required by the building regulations — in actual fact most five-foot ways are six to seven feet in width — the idea was to provide a continuous covered walkway on both sides of a street, protecting pedestrians from both the sun and the rain. Modern Singapore's colonial founder, Thomas Stamford Bingley Raffles, was the man who wrote the five-foot way in the shophouse constitution in his famous Ordinances of 4 November 1822 in which he drew up a town plan for his fledgling settlement and determined that "each house should have a verandah of a certain depth, open at all times as a continued and covered passage on each side of the street" (see also page 89). As an idea, it was enormously influential and much copied by town planners throughout South East Asia in the 19th century.

LEFT Although covered walkways are found in many parts of China, in Singapore they were mandatory. Intrepid traveller Isabella Bird in 1883 in *The Golden Chersonese and The Way Thither* described them as "long shady alleys" where "crowds of buyers and sellers chaffer over their goods, the Chinese shopkeepers asking a little more than they mean to take ...". Here, we see five-foot-ways in Amoy Street (above) and Little India (below).

OPPOSITE Blair Road (top), Everton Road (bottom left) and Bussorah Street (bottom right).

TOP  Five-foot-ways are often enlivend by decorative details. On the door of this house on Everton Road, the calligraphy reads *shou shan fu hai*, which literally means "mountain of longevity and ocean of luck".

LEFT  Blair Road five-foot-way.

OPPOSITE  A vendor of a funerary shop, Joo Chiat Road, displays wares on the five-foot-way (top left); Koon Seng Road (top right); Keong Saik Road (bottom).

# THE SHOP

The front room on the ground floor of a typical shophouse opened directly onto the five-foot way, a feature that is also characteristic of

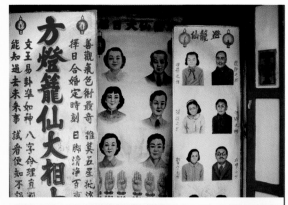

shops in mainland China. Merchandise was displayed on timber shelves and cabinets from the floor to ceiling, but invariably spilled out onto the five-foot way as well. The latter, though ostensibly a public thoroughfare, was privately owned and therefore seen by shopkeepers as a legitimate extension of their premises. The colonial authorities were forever trying to enforce legislation to keep these pedestrian walkways free from obstruction, but then, as now, they met with little success and on more than one occasion their attempts to clear Singapore's sidewalks ended in violent altercations, the most famous instance of this being the so-called "verandah riots" of 1888.

The shopkeeper served his customers from behind a long wooden counter, situated either at the back of the shop or along one side. At the end of the day, the goods on display on the five-foot way were brought inside and vertical shutters placed across the front of the shop to close up the premises for the night. In the earliest period, these shutters were inserted individually, with a crossbar, supported by brackets, to secure them in place. Later, this form of shuttering was replaced by hinged concertina doors that could be folded back on themselves during the day.

LEFT TOP  The five-foot-way experience was (and sometimes still is) entertaining for its hand-painted advertising.

LEFT BOTTOM  Enticing displays of Traditional Chinese Medicine merchandise, attractively arranged on the five-foot way, bring customers to the shop.

OPPOSITE TOP  Particular streets are often dedicated to shops and businesses specialising in a particular type of commodity or service. Arab Street (shown here), for example, is famous for wholesale and retail textile businesses.

OPPOSITE BOTTOM LEFT  Custom-built, fitted cabinets are a characteristic feature of the traditional Chinese apothecary.

OPPOSITE BOTTOM RIGHT  In crowded business premises, the five-foot way can provide a useful workplace, in this instance for the preparation and packaging of edible bird's nests.

# FRONT DOORS

In the case of townhouses and non-retail businesses which didn't require the public display of goods and merchandise, the main entrance to the premises was centrally situated, with a pair of windows symmetrically placed, one on either side. The front door was double-leafed, with a rack of horizontal wooden bars (*tanglong*, see overleaf) that could be pulled across the opening by way of added security.

In the case of townhouses, there was also a pair of half-length doors, known as *pintu pagar*. Despite the Malay terminology — the words literally mean "door fence" — the *pintu pagar* is actually a Chinese import, being a traditional feature found in southern China. In closing off the lower portion of the doorway, it enables

LEFT TOP  Entrance to 41 Emerald Hill; the scroll plaque over the door reads "Dancing Phoenix" which is an auspicious reference to the woman of the household; the male counterpart would be "Flying Dragon".

LEFT BOTTOM  The characters on this signboard read *tian quan*, or "Heavenly Stream" which, one presumes, is the name of the company whose business premises lie within. However, as in the case of so many Chinese names or epithets, there is more than one level of meaning involved here, the name of the company itself being a metaphor for the hoped for riches that will come flowing in.

OPPOSITE TOP  Paper-cut door guardians, or *menshen*, which are commonly applied to the front doors of Chinese houses at the time of the Lunar New Year festival. They are variously said to be guardian spirits from the Gates of Hell, who traditionally prevent the dead from returning to haunt the living, or alternatively, two generals, historical figures, famous for subduing malevolent ghosts and demons.

OPPOSITE BOTTOM LEFT  Couplets on a door in Blair Road: "(May your) Good Fortune be as Great as the Ocean; (your) Longevity as High as a Mountain".

the main doors of the house to be kept open during the day, thereby encouraging through ventilation, while still affording privacy for the inhabitants within.

Traditionally, there would have been a wooden signboard over the door, inscribed with large Chinese characters, picked out in gold, which proclaimed the name of the business within, or, in the case of townhouses, that of the family who resided there. Often the doors themselves were also emblazoned with auspicious characters, carved in low relief — good fortune, prosperity, peace and harmony, and a long life were the usual themes. A mirror to ward off malevolent influences was invariably placed over the doorway, together with other talismanic objects — for example a pair of scissors or a miniature trident — similarly intended to prevent malign agencies from crossing the threshold. Strips of paper inscribed with magical formulae performed a similar function, while the Taoist eight trigrams symbol (*bagua*), arranged in a particular configuration known as the King Wen or Later Heaven pattern representing the cyclical nature of the universe, was believed to encourage harmonious relations at a cosmic level.

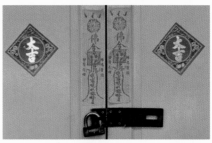

RIGHT Talismans and good-luck charms are typically placed above and on doors. Here we see the characters *da ji* meaning "Oneself will be blessed with Good Luck", along with a mirror placed over the door to prevent malevolent influences from entering the house (top). At Chinese New Year, paper talismans or good-luck charms are similarly pasted on front doors, again to ward off evil and to encourage beneficent influences to cross the threshold (third photo down). Finally, the bottom photo shows a Taoist, eight-trigram (*bagua*) symbol. Ronni Pinsler, courtesy of NAS.

OPPOSITE More doors and *pintu pagar* from Spottiswoode Park Road (top left), Everton Road (top right) and Club Street (bottom right); *tanglong* security bars in Club Street (bottom left).

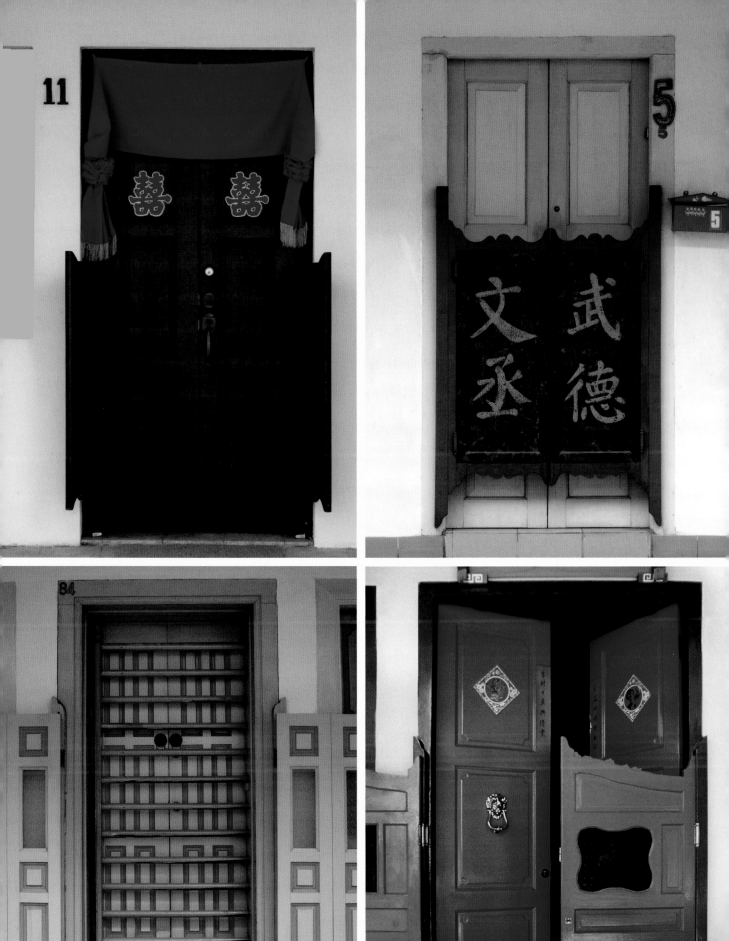

# WINDOWS

The windows on either side of the front door came with paired shutters and vertical iron bars for security. Often a rattan panel would be

inserted in the lower portion of the window, which served the same function as the *pintu pagar*, that is to say it enabled the shutters to be kept open during the day, thereby improving the flow of air through the house, while preventing prying eyes in the street from observing those within. With the introduction of glazing at the end of the 19th century, this feature was replaced by a pane of frosted glass. An air vent, about the size of a large tea tray, was let into the wall above the windows to further assist in the ventilation of the ground floor, especially when the shutters were closed at night. These were as much a decorative feature as they were a purely functional device and they came in three or four characteristic shapes that are clearly Chinese in origin.

However, for much of the 19th century, windows were no more than simple, rectangular affairs without architraves or any other form of decorative embellishment. The Mediterranean-style jalousie window was an early borrowing from European architecture — the Chinese would have first come across them in Macau and Canton in the 17th century, though the more proximal influence for Singapore builders would have been Portuguese and Dutch Malacca where a Chinese community had been resident for centuries.

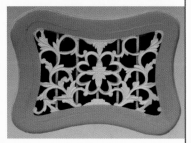

**LEFT**  Covering over a side window (top). Rattan panels inserted into the lower half of ground-floor windows provided privacy while allowing the through passage of air (middle). Traditional Chinese-style air vent over a window in Blair Road (bottom).

**OPPOSITE**  Shophouse windows are subject to an almost infinite number of different decorative permutations. The most common starting point was some sort of arrangement involving Classically-derived architraves and pilasters, with jalousie shutters, but the creative possibilities that this basic format opened up were virtually limitless. And while it is possible to create a timeline of sorts for the evolution of the shophouse window (see pages 36–37), the huge range of different styles defies categorisation.

Books of decorative paper-cuts for windows can be purchased and their lace-like patterns cut out and applied to windowpanes. The choice of images range from purely abstract designs to stylised plant or animal motifs, which as always have an auspicious significance.

Glass-fronted built-in cupboards, set into the masonry walls of the building, were a characteristic feature of well-to-do households. Resembling internal windows, they came with elaborately carved and gilded panels and surround, and served as display cabinets to show off the family heirlooms — chiefly Chinese or Peranakan porcelain, and prestige European glassware. The Chinese characters above the cabinet at top reads *he qi zhi xiang* or "Harmony causes Auspiciousness".

### Chinese Style *circa* 1880–1900
The earliest kind of window embellishment involved mainly traditional Chinese decorative elements — *chien nien* mosaic friezes, plaster reliefs featuring Chinese motifs, and wall plaques with auspicious characters.

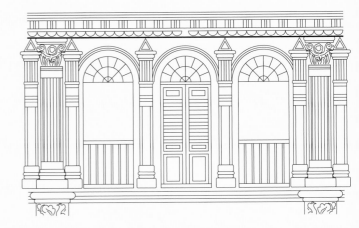

### Baroque Style 1895–1910
The Baroque window, on the other hand, was almost wholly Classical in inspiration, though sometimes local artisans were liable to add their own interpretations, which led to some strange innovations and peculiarly local embellishments.

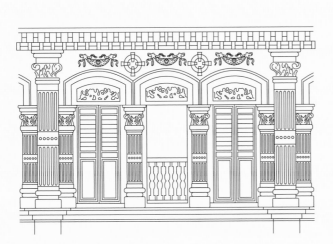

### Rococo Style 1916–1929
Conversely, the Rococo style moved in the opposite direction, the general idea being to cover every square inch of the façade with as much ornamentation as possible — swags, garlands, festoons, and, later, traditional Chinese plant and animal motifs.

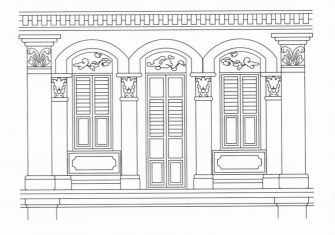

### East Coast Peranakan Style 1920–1935
The rise of the East Coast suburbs between the wars saw the introduction of a more subdued Rococo style, which at times bordered on the Neo-Classical, but still retained some sort of amusement in the form Chinese animal and plant motifs.

## Jubilee Style 1898–1906

Jubilee was another kind of Baroque style which flourished briefly at the turn of the last century, but was more three-dimensional, with ponderous, heavily sculpted features, executed in the round.

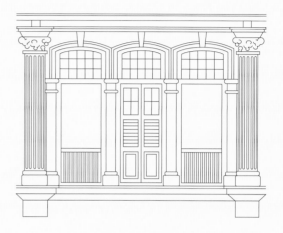

## Neo-Classical Style *circa* 1910–1930

The Neo-Classical style came about almost in reaction to the monumental Jubilee style, favouring lighter, more delicate decorative reliefs and a generally less cluttered arrangement of the facade.

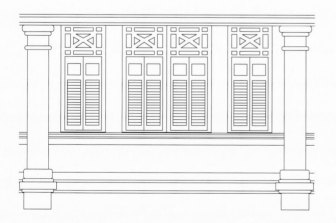

## Stripped Classical Style 1925–1930

The Stripped Classical style reduced Classical details to their essentials, a kind of process of progressive abstraction which ultimately led to the Modernist movement.

## Modernist Style 1933–1941

The Modernist window was based on strictly rationalist principles. There were no more twiddly bits, just steel-framed casement windows and the very minimum of detailing, though elements like sun visors, or *brise soleil*, were at once practical and stylish at the same time.

# CHINESE DECORATIVE ELEMENTS

Even in the earliest days of settlement, when the Singapore shophouse was at its most perfunctory stage of development, there is evidence of attempts to enliven the façade of buildings with a bit of colour and surface decoration. Thus, French naval officer, Lieutenant (later Admiral) François-Edmond Pâris, whose ship, the corvette *La Favourite*, put in to Singapore in 1831, was able to comment on how "the Chinese merchants, who take care of all the lesser business deals, decorate their houses with the bizarre taste which is typical of their nation", noting that "the façades are covered with brightly coloured frescoes".

Despite such assertions, the surviving pictorial record — watercolours, engravings, early photographs and the like — shows the early Singapore shophouse as a pretty prosaic affair. There may have been some sort of simple moulding to mark the transition between the ground floor and the commencement of the floor above and an equally modest cornice beneath the eaves. Otherwise, that was pretty much about it by way of architectural detailing.

However, by the last quarter of the 19th century, increasing confidence in Singapore's future as a prosperous entrepôt and centre of regional trade encouraged many wealthy Chinese merchants and businessmen to consider making the British Settlement their permanent home. Up until this time, most immigrants from mainland China had arrived in Singapore fully intending to return to their ancestral villages one day, though for most, this was a never-to-be-realised dream. For second generation Chinese, however — that is to say, those who had been born in Singapore and whose families were evidently prospering there — the situation was rather different. It was Singapore that was

**LEFT** Scroll plaque over a window head in Duxton Hill; the characters signify *long fei* or "Flying Dragon" an auspicious reference to male members of the household (see also page 28). Over its paired window, the other side of the door, the characters read *feng wu* ("Dancing Phoenix").

**OPPOSITE TOP** Chinoiserie-style façade, Kitchener Road, late 1920s.

**OPPOSITE BOTTOM** Mosaic *chien nien* creatures in Mohamed Sultan Road. Chinese representations of animals can be a little imaginative to say the least, particularly when it comes to elephants; often one is left puzzling as to precisely what kind of beast one is looking at.

properly their home, not the distant land of their forefathers, which they had seldom visited, if at all, and they were more inclined to stay put. With this in mind, those who had money to play around with were happy to show off their wealth through their houses, spending much more on decorative features and the quality of materials used than had hitherto been the case.

The principal source of inspiration in this early phase of ornamentation still came from mainland China and usually took the form of stucco reliefs and painted decorative panels or plaques depicting traditional Chinese themes — flowers and fruit, birds and bamboo, landscapes, acts of filial piety and other morally-uplifting vignettes, as well as scenes drawn from folk tales, literature and Chinese opera.

Other traditional Chinese features include granite thresholds and window cills; sculpted wooden beams and corbels, the details picked out in gold leaf; latticework screens and elaborately carved door- and window-panels; green-glazed airbricks and bamboo-shaped ceramic window mullions. Chinese-style canopy roofs over the five-foot way were another popular feature and they were typically surmounted by a decorative frieze comprising a mosaic of coloured ceramic shards cemented over bas-reliefs of flowers or animals to create a colourful, multifaceted surface. Appropriately, the technique is known as *chien nien*, meaning literally 'to cut and paste', and was very popular in Canton in the 1870s.

By the turn of the last century these Chinese decorative features had been augmented, even superseded, by Western Classical elements (Part 2), but in the 1920s there was a revival of enthusiasm for traditional Chinese imagery with shophouse façades being almost overwhelmed in some instances by a profusion of animal and plant motifs.

OPPOSITE The early shophouse facade was a fairly straightforward affair in terms of ornamentation, but as the 19th century progressed, decorative elements became increasingly prevalent. Typically, the shophouse façade was divided into three bays, each filled by a window, but while the central window was almost invariably a full length, floor-to-ceiling affair, as often as not the cill of the windows on either side was waist height, allowing a decorative stucco panel to be placed beneath each window. These featured traditional Chinese motifs or little vignettes in relief of amusing scenes from everyday life or literary themes. Similarly, there was often a stucco plaque with some kind of auspicious text in Chinese characters over the top of the windows; often the characters would themselves be in relief.

THIS PAGE Green-glaze ceramic bamboo mullions in a circular aperture in a forecourt wall, Blair Road (above left). Confronting Chinoiserie dragons at the junction of Joo Chiat Road and Joo Chiat Place (top). Five-foot way at 165 Telok Ayer Street (above).

# WESTERN ARCHITECTURAL INFLUENCES

Western influences first begin to make an appearance in the shophouse repertoire in the mid-1880s in the form of Classical details lifted from colonial architecture — the offices and warehouses of the major European merchant houses located in and around Raffles Place provided a useful starting point in this respect.

Georgian-style fanlights, augmented by simple Classical mouldings in the Roman Doric style, were early acquisitions, but it wasn't long before the shophouse façade literally erupted into a dazzling display of surface ornamentation. Fluted pilasters surmounted by Corinthian capitals divided up the façade into bays, while elaborate architraves framed the window openings, with a keystone, perhaps, at the head. Chinese reliefs gave way to Classical friezes and dentilated cornices, with a pediment or some sort of cartouche on top to finish the whole thing off. There may have been scant respect for the correct use of Classical orders and proportions, but interestingly a local aesthetic, with its own implicit rules and principals, soon emerged, and by the end of the 19th century one can discern a clearly recognisable 'school' of Classically-influenced shophouse architecture, usually referred to

LEFT  Chinese-Baroque was at its height in the first decade of the 20th century. This three-storey corner building, which was designed in 1908 by perhaps the greatest of shophouse Classicists, Wee Teck Moh, is almost wholly European in inspiration with its fluted Corinthian pilasters, Venetian windows and dentiled cornices.

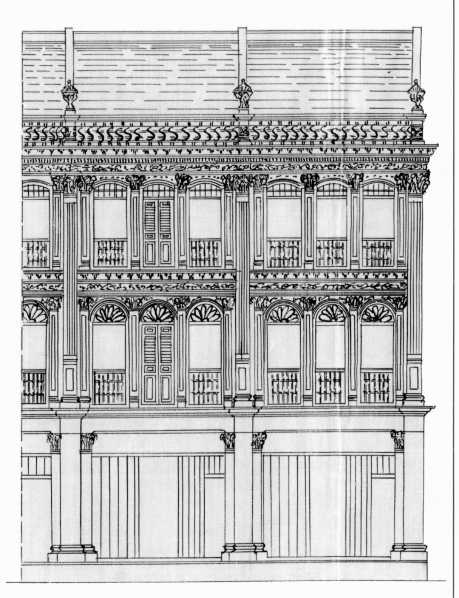

Variations on a theme: Initial appearances can be deceptive and what might appear at first glance to be a quite straightforward terrace of Baroque-style shophouses can, on closer inspection, reveal unexpected flights of fancy on the part of the Chinese artisans who were responsible for the stucco detailing. In these two examples from Duxton Hill (below) and Purvis Street (bottom), we find a happy mix of Chinese and Classical elements — pomegranates and acanthus-leaf capitals, fire-breathing dragons and a dentiled cornice; Chinese Baroque in every sense of the term!

ABOVE Five shophouses for Messrs Ho Hin & Co at Tanjong Pagar Road, Wee Teck Moh, 1901. 1901 was the year that saw the beginning of a major redevelopment of Tanjong Pagar Road, which was the main thoroughfare leading from the town to the docks, with older two-storey shophouses being replaced by prestige developments like this one — three-storey Baroque sentinels, lining both sides of the road, which no doubt were intended to impress new arrivals as they proceeded from their ship to the great metropolis. BCA Collection, courtesy of NAS.

OPPOSITE The Classical repertoire gave local artisans plenty of scope for their creative imaginings. Swags and escutcheons, medallions and *fleur-de-lys*, egg-and-dart and acanthus leaves, were all joyfully seized upon and reproduced with varying degrees of faithfulness to the original.

BELOW Dried Goods Guild Hall, Ann Siang Hill, 1940; cutting-edge tropical Deco from W T (Wee Tuck) Foo (see page 146). Foo, who was active from the mid-1920s onwards, was one of Singapore's leading local Modernists in the years before the outbreak of the war in the Pacific. BCA Collection, courtesy of NAS.

as Chinese Baroque — the term was coined by Northcote Parkinson, of Parkinson's Law fame, who was Raffles Professor of History at the University of Malaya in the 1950s.

These Classical details, were built up from a combination of specially manufactured bricks, which provided the underlying structure over which a thick layer of stucco was applied. The latter could be sculpted *in situ* before it set, but standard decorative elements such as capitals and other ornamental motifs were pre-cast in wooden moulds and then fixed in place. This stucco was again made up from sand and lime, in the same way as the plaster used for walls, but was reinforced with white of eggs, horse hair and a coarse, unrefined sugar drawn from palms, mixed with water in which coconut husks had been steeped. The recipe for this locally-manufactured stucco, or Madras *chunam* as it was known, was introduced from British India; not only was it cheap to produce, but it was also incredibly hard-wearing.

The Classically-influenced shophouse passed through several stylistic phases, eventually morphing into a kind of Rococo, "wedding cake" style of architecture around the time of World War I. The latter remained popular until the end of the 1920s, at which point one sees more contemporary European influences — both Art Deco and Modernist — entering the shophouse repertoire, along with the adoption of new materials and building technologies: reinforced-concrete and steel joists, metal-framed windows, with green-tinted glass, terrazzo floors, Shanghai plaster and artificial stone finishes. This was the last phase in the evolution of the Singapore shophouse and it was one that had a surprising longevity, surviving well into the post-war era and into the early years of independence.

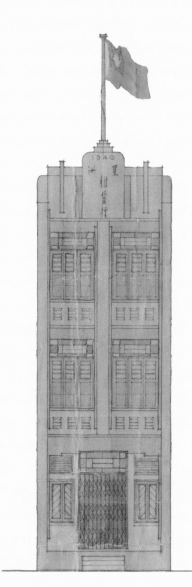

# COURTYARDS
# AND SKYWELLS

Courtyards are a quintessential feature of traditional Chinese architecture. Be it a temple or a palace, a mansion or farmhouse — all have, at their centre, a courtyard or *yuanzi*. Shophouses are no different in this respect, except that the courtyard here is very much reduced in size, often comprising little more than an airwell, or "skywell" (*tianjing*) as the Chinese more poetically call them. Airwell or skywell, this little patch of open space nevertheless remains a crucial element in the composition of the traditional Chinese shophouse.

At a purely functional level, it brought light to the interior of what would otherwise have been a very dark building, and, at the same time, it also assisted in natural ventilation by allowing warm air from inside the building to escape which in turn encouraged the flow of air through the interior — the basic principle is that of a flue or chimney. Lastly, it provided a cool and quiet refuge from the hustle and bustle of the noisy streets outside, a pleasant place of retreat from the world at large; in this respect it fulfilled a function similar to that of the patio in traditional Spanish architecture.

RIGHT  Fountains and fishponds, often fed by rainwater collected from the roof, were a popular feature for skywells in the houses of the rich. Fish are an auspicious creature in traditional Chinese culture, because the word for "fish", *yu*, is a pronounced the same as the term for "abundance", in other words wealth. Fish also symbolize harmony, marital happiness and reproduction because they multiply rapidly and sometimes swim in pairs. Flowing water is also meant, by association, to encourage a sense of balance or harmony in one's life; the idea is related to the Taoist concept of *wu wei* — passivity, calm, non-striving, humility, and a lack of planning — literally "going with the flow", for to plan is to go against the Tao.

In many respects the Chinese skywell is very like the atrium in a Roman villa. In the case of the Roman villa, the paved floor of the atrium was recessed in relation to the floors of the surrounding rooms and acted as a kind of shallow well, or *impluvium*, which collected the rainfall entering from above and directed it to a cistern beneath the building. One finds exactly the same system in China, except that in the case of Chinese *tianjing*, the collected rainwater did not always end up in an underground cistern but as often as not became a pond instead; the idea of water being collected inside the house is an auspicious one in the Chinese way of thinking, flowing water being associated with the idea of accumulating wealth.

# SHRINES AND ALTARS

Maintaining good relations with the gods and ancestors are key considerations in traditional Chinese culture and these concerns are reflected in the organisation of domestic space within the shophouse. The front room of a shop- or townhouse corresponds to the southern entrance pavilion in the Chinese courtyard house and this is where one traditionally would find an altar dedicated to the household deity, placed at the far end, directly facing the front door. The altar might be no more than a red-painted wall shelf with an image of the deity and enough space for a bowl of offerings and a joss-stick holder, but in the homes of wealthier families, the altar would typically comprise a sculpture of the deity placed on a lacquered altar table, ornamented with bird and animal carvings and a floral frieze highlighted in gold leaf. This would be flanked by scrolls or carved wooden plaques with calligraphy extolling the various merits of the household god — typically Guan Yin, the goddess of mercy, or else quasi-mythical figures from popular Taoist belief such as the three heroic blood-brothers of the Warring States period, Guan Gong, Zhang Fei and Liu Bei, renowned for their chivalry, courage and righteousness. The presence of this altar, so positioned, was believed to protect the occupants of the house from misfortune and to safeguard against malevolent influences entering the house.

LEFT  In smaller houses, where there is no rear hall corresponding to the ancestral pavilion in a courtyard house, the family altar and the shrine dedicated to the household gods may either be combined, or else, as in this instance, the family altar may be relocated to the back wall of the front room upstairs.

OPPOSITE TOP  Family altar in a Chinese shophouse in Hoi Ann, Vietnam. In modern times, ancestral tablets have often been superseded by photographs of the deceased.

OPPOSITE BOTTOM  Altar dedicated to household gods, River Valley Road.

ABOVE  Stand alone Thai Buddhist shrine in a Katong terrace.

OPPOSITE TOP  This "family" altar at Sian Teck Tng Vegetarian Convent is dedicated to the principal benefactor and former mother superior (*kor tai*) as opposed to specific ancestors.

OPPOSITE MIDDLE LEFT  Shrine dedicated to the Earth God, Tu Di Gong, who like so many Chinese deities is generally associated with the conference of wealth and prosperity, traditionally in an agricultural context. The altar is usually placed on the ground beside the front door or entrance to a building.

OPPOSITE MIDDLE RIGHT  Altar dedicated to Tua Pek Kong, a very local Singaporean and Malaysian deity, who is also associated with the accumulation of wealth.

OPPOSITE BOTTOM LEFT  Another shrine dedicated to the gods of fiscal prosperity, with porcelain figurines of Tua Pek Kong (left) and Tian Kuan Tze Fu, the God of Wealth (right).

OPPOSITE BOTTOM RIGHT  An altar at the home of a traditional healer in Pegu Road.

The basis of ancestor worship in traditional Chinese society rests on an underlying belief that deceased family members not only continue to take an interest in the affairs of the world, but also have the ability to influence the lives and fortunes of their descendents. For this reason, an altar dedicated to the family's ancestors was always erected in the most auspicious location within the domestic compound, which in the traditional Chinese courtyard house, would have been the main hall, or *zhengwu*, situated on the north side of the courtyard. In the case of shophouses and townhouses, the family altar is usually situated along the back wall of the innermost hall — that is to say, the room on the far side of the airwell as one proceeds towards the rear of the building, which corresponds morphologically to the main hall in a courtyard house.

The family altar typically comprises a tall, narrow table positioned against the back wall of the main hall. This is where the ancestral shrine is placed, the latter often taking the form of a miniature house, made from wood, complete with doors, latticework panels, columns and a tiled roof. Inside are placed the family's ancestral tablets, each inscribed with the name of a former family member who has passed on. Offerings of fruit and little bowls of tea are put before the shrine, together with lighted joss sticks, usually on a daily basis. This is where rites of passage marking key stages in the lives of family members — births, deaths, coming of age ceremonies, marriages and so on — are celebrated, as well as the major festivities in the Chinese lunar calendar, the most important of these being that of Chinese New Year. In this respect, the Chinese house is at once a family home and also its principal place of worship, a kind of private sanctum where family members come together to observe the major and minor ceremonials of Chinese religious life, united in their sense of common purpose and shared ancestral ties.

Sometimes, especially in smaller premises, the family shrine and altar to the household deities may be combined, in which case there is often a second altar table, called the *ba xian* or "Eight Immortals" table, which fits beneath the high altar, in order to accommodate the extra offerings and ritual paraphernalia.

# FLOOR TILES AND
## PAVING STONES

Locally-made clay floor tiles, roughly 15 inches square (100 sq cm), known as "Malacca tiles", were used for the ground floor of the Singapore shophouse and to pave the five-foot way. They were set in a bed of lime mortar which allowed evaporation from the damp earth beneath, cooling the ground floor rooms in the process. Later, patterned encaustic tiles (see overleaf) imported from Europe were used in their place, the encaustic floor tile being popular in Victorian England from the 1860s onwards. Unpolished granite slabs, quarried locally on the nearby island of Pulau Ubin, were used for heel stones, thresholds, trimming and as paving stones for airwells.

LEFT  Terracotta Malacca tiles, Heeren Street (Jalan Tun Tan Cheng Lock), Malacca.

BELOW LEFT  Lion-faced granite heel stone.

BELOW AND OPPOSITE  In the wealthier neighbourhoods such as Emerald Hill and other up market residential neighbourhoods such as Blair Plain (following pages), Victorian-style encaustic floor tiles were used for the five-foot ways.

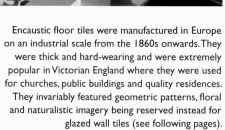

Encaustic floor tiles were manufactured in Europe on an industrial scale from the 1860s onwards. They were thick and hard-wearing and were extremely popular in Victorian England where they were used for churches, public buildings and quality residences. They invariably featured geometric patterns, floral and naturalistic imagery being reserved instead for glazed wall tiles (see following pages).

In the examples here, it is interesting to note that all the floral patterns have eight-petalled flowers; eight, or *fa*, translates as "prosperity". The same symbolism is often found in the octagonal shape of the tiles.

# GLAZED CERAMIC TILES

Decorative ceramic tiles — the sort of tiles that were used in latter half of the Victorian era as a surround for the fireplace and hearth in thousands of suburban houses across the British Isles — were popular from the late 19th century through to the early years of the 20th century when we find a lot of tiles with Art Nouveau motifs. Initially these decorative wall tiles were employed for interiors — typically they were applied to the wall space between the floor and a waist-height dado rail — but around the time of World War I they began to be used for external surfaces, as decorative panels beneath windows, both at street level and on the floors above. Unlike the pavement tiles used for floors and the five-foot way verandahs, these decorative wall tiles were glazed and often in relief. And whereas floor tiles almost always featured geometric designs, wall tiles tended to feature floral motifs which no doubt appealed to traditional Chinese aesthetic sensibilities.

The great majority of tiles date either from the Victorian era or the first decades of the 20th century (opposite), but in later shophouses, for example those in Katong and Joo Chiat, one notices the appearance of a more contemporary kind of tile featuring more naturalistic representations of birds and flowers (left).

Ceramic tiles were never more popular that in the late 1920s, as these examples from Syed Alwi Road (opposite and above) and Jiak Chuan Road (middle) illustrate. Even temples were not exempt from the craze, as can be seen here in Keong Saik Road (right).

OVERLEAF  The ceramic-fronted shophouse reaches its apotheosis in this astonishing terrace of 18 townhouses at Petain Road which date from 1930. They are all the more remarkable for having been designed by British architect, E V Miller, who, if left to his own devices, was an out-and-out Modernist in the Bauhaus tradition; no doubt the wishes of his client, one Mohamed bin Haji Omar, had something to do with achieving this end result.

# STRUCTURAL TIMBERS AND SCREENS

The main structural timbers of the shophouse — bressummers, beams, floor joists and roof purlins — were from naturally occurring tropical hardwoods (mainly Dipterocarps) from the forests of Singapore and the Malay peninsula. The most commonly used varieties were *balau* (*Shorea* spp), *bintangor* (*Calophyllum* spp), *daru-daru* (*Planchonella* spp), *rassak* (*Vatica rassak*), and *tempinis* (*Strebulous elongates*), which seemed to have been employed more or less interchangeably for the different house parts; floorboards were usually made from planks of *seraya* (*Shorea* spp).

ABOVE Traditional Chinese bracket and beam construction methods were not usually necessary for the roofs of shophouses where the narrow width of the building was sufficient to allow the purlins to span the interval between party walls unsupported. One does find them, however, in prestige buildings such as the Ying Fo Fui Clan Association in Telok Ayer Street (above) or Towkay Tan Yeok Nee's courtyard house on Clemenceau Avenue (overleaf).

OPPOSITE These beautifully carved front doors and entrance screen, which can be found at 98 Emerald Hill, were originally from Malacca, but were brought to their new home by poet and playwright, the late Dr Goh Peng Swee, who lived in this house in the 1980s. Malacca, being one of the oldest Chinese Nanyang communities is a rich repository of Peranakan architectural treasures, many of which have found their way to Singapore to be installed in the homes of local antique collectors.

The main walls of a shophouse were masonry, except in out of town areas where a combination of brick piers and plank walls was often used, the potentially disastrous consequences of fire being considerably lessened away from the city. Interior walls and partitions, on the other hand, were usually timber. In the case of the most ordinary sort of shophouse, these internal divisions were simple stud walls with wood or plank panels, which were usually continued up from the floor to within a couple of feet of the ceiling, the remaining portion then being filled by simple latticework to encourage the circulation of air within the building. In the houses of the well-to-do, on the other hand, these internal partitions were often turned into works of art — elaborately carved timber screens and panels, pierced by intricate fretwork or geometric-patterned latticework to traditionally Chinese designs, and dripping with lacquer and gold leaf.

Like the external ornamentation of the shophouse, the decorative motifs on these screens featured birds, plants and animals, or perhaps a tableau of figures depicting themes of filial

piety and other morally upstanding values close to the Chinese heart. As well as providing an opportunity for displaying dazzling artistry and craftsmanship, these screens, with their lattices and fretwork panels, helped to encourage the circulation of air within the building, assisted by the chimney-like pull of the skywell or internal courtyard. Corbels and roof brackets provided other opportunities for elaborate woodcarving which was usually carried out by Chinese artisans, either locally, or, if one could afford it, by specially commissioned master craftsmen back in China.

ABOVE Peranakan *pintu pagar* and entrance screen, again retrieved from Malacca and installed in a house on River Valley Road.

LEFT Chinese screen from a house in Emerald Hill. Despite the traditional enthusiasm for naturalistic motifs — birds, beasts and flowers — Chinese craftsmen were also adept at complicated abstract designs and pattern making, which have an equally long history back in ancient China.

OPPOSITE TOP AND MIDDLE Timber floorboards and joists from Blair Road (top) and Katong (middle).

OPPOSITE BOTTOM Lion bracket, Tan Yeok Nee Mansion, Clemenceau Avenue. Lions, though not so highly regarded as tigers in Chinese culture and folklore, are generally accorded a protective influence.

# MALAY INFLUENCES

Malay influences enter the shophouse vocabulary in relation to decorative woodwork. They were found not so much in the interior screens

and panelling which usually were executed by traditional Chinese artisans, but rather in the fretted facia boards under the roof eaves and so-called Peranakan-style window tracery.

The Malay fondness for fretted eaves boards and associated decorative features such as barge boards, roof finials and serrated ridge pieces, owed a lot to Victorian architectural ornamentation of the mid to late 19th century. These supposedly "Gothick" decorative elements were a standard part of the repertoire of the English revivalist Arts and Crafts movement, but they also seemed to strike some deep-seated emotion in Malay aesthetic sensibilities and it wasn't long before they were appropriated for the Malay house.

In relation to the Singapore house, fretted eaves boards were popular in domestic architecture from at least the 1860s onwards, but they didn't cross over into shophouse architecture in a major way until after World War I. One typically finds them in predominantly Malay areas like Kampong Glam or the Peranakan-populated suburbs of Katong.

Malay-style tracery in place of glazed lights for the heads of shophouse windows goes back much further, to around the turn of the last century. The original inspiration again seems to have been the Malay house where extensive use is made of fretted

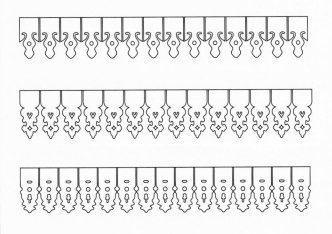

grilles and screens to enhance natural the ventilation of the building. Quite possibly the original commissions came from Peranakan families — those long-established mixed-race descendents of early Chinese settlers in the region with a hybrid Sino-Malay cultural heritage — and no doubt Malay craftsmen were employed in their production. However, by the beginning of the 1920s, Peranakan lights were on an equal footing with glazing in terms of their popularity and there seems to be no clear-cut division between the deployment of this decorative feature and occupants of the building. By this time, Georgian-style fanlights had disappeared from the scene altogether.

# LOGGIAS

In the 19th century, a top floor loggia was a popular addition to Chinese-style townhouses. In essence, this was a balustraded terrace over-looking the street with a traditional Chinese roof placed over the top of it. The latter was a separate structure from the main roof of the building and usually came with "crawling cat" gables at either end.

Classical, arcaded first-floor loggias, typically with green-glaze Venetian balusters and Romanesque arches supported on truncated Doric or Corinthian columns in the round, made an appearance around the turn of the century in conjunction with the then popular Jubilee style (see pages 116–117). They then slipped from favour for a while but made a return at the outbreak of World War I. As before, they were placed directly over the five-foot way and were typically colonnaded structures with glazing inserted into the arches to afford some protection from the rain.

Loggias are primarily associated with townhouses, rather than shophouses *per se*, and came to be a characteristic feature of residential architecture between the wars — the loggia was a favourite device of Eurasian architect J B Westerhout (see page 139).

LEFT  Loggia at Blair Road. Like the colonial verandah, the loggia acted as a kind of sun visor, casting a shadow over the external wall of the upper floor of the shophouse during the hottest part of the day and thereby reducing the warming effect of solar radiation. At the same time, it created an agreeable indoor-outdoor space for relaxing and indulging in horticultural pursuits. Lastly, it served as a useful communication corridor between different rooms on the upper floor.

OPPOSITE  The loggia was open to a number of interpretations. The earliest type was the Chinese pavilion style at the turn of the last century — Mohamed Sultan Street (top) and Club Street (bottom right). Then there was the Venetian Renaissance style, as found at Blair Road (middle, left) and Neil Road (bottom left). Finally we get the classic late-1920s version as seen at Rowell Road (middle right).

# INTERNAL STAIRCASES

Shophouse staircases were made of timber with wooden newel posts and lathe-turned banisters and handrails. The first few stairs were usually set on brick foundations to prevent them from coming into contact with wet floors; in the townhouses of the wealthy, they would have constituted slabs of granite, signifying permanence and strength. In the latter instance, the banisters would also be more ornate with the ornamental features picked out in gold leaf. Sometimes prefabricated cast-iron spiral staircases were fitted, since they were not only decorative, but also economical in terms of their use of space.

Staircases ranged from the purely functional, which employed standard, lathe-turned Victorian banisters, to highly ornate Chinese affairs, with lion-headed newel posts and intricate fretwork banisters as seen at Emerald Hill (opposite, bottom right). The base of the stairs, which was usually constructed from brick, was often turned into a decorative feature such as here at Neil Road (above). In the same house, there is also a handsome wrought-iron spiral staircase that was installed after the house was renovated (right).

# EXTERNAL STAIRCASES

External pre-cast concrete spiral staircases make their appearance at the rear of shophouses from the mid-1920s onwards and represent an early example of prefabricated modular construction techniques — each individual stair was cast as a separate unit and all one had to do was to simply place one unit on top of another until one arrived at the desired height.

The reason for their introduction was due to two interrelated factors. First, the increasing numbers of new shophouses that were purpose-built as tenement housing in the period immediately after World War 1; and secondly, the implementation of a backlanes programme to facilitate the collection of night-soil from shophouses that were not connected to the sewerage system (and at that time very few were).

Quite simply, the staircases were there to enable the night-soil *wallah* to enter from the backlane and collect used night-soil pails from the upper storeys of tenement dwellings without having to pass through the main body of the building. Despite being no more than a pragmatic solution to one of the most basic problems in domestic architecture, these staircases are quite interesting structures in their own right, as well as being a quintessential feature of the Singapore shophouse between the wars.

Though mass-produced, there was actually quite a lot of variation to the pre-cast concrete staircase, which mainly had to do with the decorative treatment of the balustrading as can be seen here. Different manufacturers came up with patterns as can be seen from our three examples.

# KITCHENS

The kitchen was typically located on the ground floor, at the back, with meals being cooked on a charcoal hearth, or *dapur* (the word is Malay). This was a waist-high, brick structure, with a series of small chambers let into the sides into which sticks of charcoal could be fed. Meanwhile, the tiled upper surface had circular holes of different sizes cut into it which were designed to receive the convex bottom of a wok.

Food was kept in a gauze-fronted cabinet, or meat-safe, whose legs were placed in little bowls of water to stop the ants crawling up, while perishables were kept in a zinc-lined ice box, though only the well-to-do were likely to indulge in such extravagances.

The rear of the house was also the "wet" area, where clothes were washed and members of the household performed their ablutions, the latter in an enclosed bathhouse where the washing facilities comprised a large Shanghai jar with a dipper floating in it. In the 19th century, every house had its own well and household wells continued to be widely used long after the Municipality introduced a piped water system to the city, beginning in 1878.

The privy was enclosed in a separate cubicle and usually consisted of little more than a raised floor with a hole in it and a bucket placed beneath. Responsibility for the removal and disposal of night soil was left in the hands of private Chinese contractors who would arrange for its collection every three days; they made a little extra money by selling the stuff on to market gardeners on the edge of town who used it as manure for their crops. In 1911, the Municipality drew up plans for a modern water-carriage sewerage system but it was not until well after World War 11 that this was fully operational.

LEFT ABOVE  Kitchens on the ground floor were open-sided, which made for a pleasant place to prepare food.

LEFT BELOW AND OPPOSITE TOP  Traditional Chinese-style kitchens; note the charcoal-burning brick hearths.

ABOVE LEFT The kitchen at the Sian Teck Tng Convent at Cuppage Terrace with huge woks nestling in circular apertures cut in the top of the brick *dapur*. Note the altar to the kitchen god, Zao Jun, on the wall to the right.

ABOVE RIGHT A pretty Peranakan lass in a tight-fitting *sarong kebaya* stirs up a delicious repast that could choke a pig, in a fabulously-appointed, retro-shophouse kitchen. *Enak enak!*

# BEDROOMS

The bedrooms were always located upstairs and were primarily identified as female spaces. In the homes of wealthy families, they were somewhere that women could retire to in order to get on with their work, such as embroidery or the making of clothes, or else indulge in female leisure activities, including socialising with other women in the household. As well as a place for sleeping or female retreat, this inner space was also reserved for the intimacies of family life. Whereas downstairs, relations between men and women within the extended family were carefully prescribed, upstairs, in their inner sanctum, women were free to let their hair down, both literally and metaphorically, enjoying their husband's company and that of their children in a free and socially unconstrained setting.

In Peranakan homes special emphasis was placed on the bridal chamber which was situated at the front of the house, directly over the reception hall. Though seldom seen by outsiders, no expense was spared on the decoration of this space. Peter Lee and Jennifer Chen, authors of *Rumah Baba: Life in a Peranakan House*, describe the bridal chamber as "the quintessential symbol of a family's wealth and status". Special attention was paid to the matrimonial bed, an elaborately carved, four-poster affair, gilded with gold leaf or inlaid with mother of pearl. This was usually commissioned from traditional craftsmen in China and then shipped over to Singapore; at a later period, though, English brass beds became fashionable, as a symbol of the cosmopolitan outlook of progressive Peranakan families who in their alternative guise as Straits Chinese, were often members of the ruling elite.

TOP  Peranakan, mother-of-pearl inlaid bridal bed, acquired from Penang, in the house of Johnson Tan on River Valley Road.

ABOVE  Tropical Edwardian four-poster brass bed, with fitted mosquito nets, at the Baba House on Neil Road.

OPPOSITE  Peranakan bridal bed, Baba House, Neil Road. Wealthy Babas traditionally spent a fortune on the nuptials of their children. Peranakan marriages as often as not were matrilocal — that is to say, the groom went to live in his wife's household — and even if they were not, the bridegroom was expected to spend the wedding night and several nights following at his wife's house. Accordingly, the bridal bed was decorated in the most lavish manner with embroidered silk drapes and hung about with talismans to encourage a long and happy life together, and of course many children.

# ROOFS AND ROOF TILES

In the case of roof tiles, a distinction should be made here between locally manufactured roof tiles and those imported from China. The original inspiration for Chinese roof tiles seems to have come from nature and the use of halved bamboo stems, laid in a pattern of alternating and overlapping ridges and furrows, as an ancient roofing material. Reconstituted in clay, this kind of roofing, with local variations, is recorded as early as the 6th century BC. The type of Chinese roof tile that we see in Singapore was imported from southern China and comprises a bottom layer of broad, slightly concave tiles, laid side by side on battens, with an upper layer of narrower, convex tiles, semicircular in section, placed over the joints. This kind of roof tile is usually only found in temples and prestige dwellings like the Tan Yeok Nee mansion (see pages 94–97). In the case of shophouses, they were only used for the little ornamental canopy roof, supported on granite brackets, which extends over the five-foot way at the first storey level; the main roof was covered in smaller, v-shaped tiles that were manufactured locally.

Somewhat confusingly, the latter are referred to on working drawings as "Chinese tiles", no doubt on account of the fact that they were produced by largely Chinese manufactories (by the same token locally manufactured bricks were referred to in the 19th century as "Chinese bricks"). They actually seem to be of Portuguese origin and were introduced to the region in the early 16th century, which is when Chinese artisans first became acquainted with their manufacture being called upon to produce them in large numbers for the Portuguese in Malacca.

Generically, they belong to what is known today as the tapered Missionary type. The term derives from Spanish Mission architecture in the US and belies its Iberian origin, though ultimately this kind of roof tile goes back to Roman times. In principle, such tiles function in exactly the same way as Chinese roof tiles — interlocking layers of convex and concave tiles, creating a series of ridges and furrows to expedite the run off of rainwater. The tiles are slightly tapered, being a little narrower at the top end than at their base, which ensures a snug fit and helps keep them in place on the sloping plane of a pitched roof.

ABOVE  Modern reproduction "Peranakan" tiles, made in France.

OPPOSITE TOP  Traditional Chinese-tile roof at Towkay Tan Yeok Nee's courtyard house on Clemenceau Avenue. The original tiles would have been imported from China.

OPPOSITE BOTTOM  Renovated roofs in Kim Yam Road, refurbished with modern v-shaped "Chinese tiles", with the original behind in Tong Watt Street.

# DEVELOPMENT OF THE SHOPHOUSE

2

# ORIGINS OF THE SHOPHOUSE

The origins of the Singapore shophouse ultimately lie in China and it is in China that any examination of the shophouse as an architectural tradition must naturally begin. The archetypal Chinese residence is of course the courtyard house or *siheyuan*, but two points need to be made here. Firstly, that fully-realised courtyard houses were only an option for wealthier families, and secondly, for all the homogeneity and consistency of traditional Chinese architecture, there are significant regional differences, particularly between buildings in the north of China and those in the south. It is the architecture of China's southern provinces, and especially the two coastal provinces of Guangdong and Fujian, which especially concerns us here, for this is where the great majority of Singapore's immigrant Chinese population came from. Like most immigrant communities, they brought their customs and building traditions with them — therefore, the architecture of this region has been the major influence in defining the Singapore shophouse.

Many of the features we usually associate with the Singapore shophouse — a long and narrow plan, airwells, firewalls and even Raffles' celebrated five-foot way — are to be found in southern China where one typically encounters rows or terraces of similarly-built houses separated by narrow lanes. This type of settlement pattern encouraged the adoption of different construction methods to those of northern China, most notably load-bearing party walls into which the floor joists and roof purlins are set. The latter typically extend above the roof ridge and act as firewalls, reducing the risk of domestic conflagrations spreading from one unit to the next; this feature is rarely seen in northern China.

The long and narrow plan — a reflection of the fact that buildings in southern China were taxed according to their width or frontage on to the street — meant that the open courtyard, the defining feature of domestic architecture in the north, is very much reduced in size in southern Chinese town and village houses. Even so, it

ABOVE   Traditional village architecture in Jiangsu Province, China. Note the upper storey projecting over the ground floor to create a covered walkway, which anticipates Raffles' celebrated five-foot way.

still serves an important purpose by bringing light to the interior of what would otherwise be a very dark building, while at the same time encouraging the circulation of air within. High ceilings, ventilation grilles and lattice-like interior partitions also helped to improve the natural ventilation of the building, which was an important consideration in southern China's hot and humid sub-tropical climate.

ABOVE   Although lacking a covered walkway, or front porch, these traditional timber shophouses in Yunnan, clearly prefigure the Singapore shophouse and belie an ancient architectural tradition stretching back centuries, if not millennia.

# NANYANG COMMUNITIES

The first Chinese to arrive in Singapore came not from China but from the region round about: Malacca, Penang, Medan in Sumatra, the Javanese city-ports of Batavia, Cirebon and Surabaya, and various islands in the Riau Archipelago. In China this region was referred to as Nanyang, or the "Southern Seas", and there had been Chinese merchant communities settled there for centuries, trading in pepper, cloves and other luxury items ranging from rhinoceros horn to sandalwood, edible bird's nests and the slug-like sea cucumber or *bêche-de-mer*.

At the time of modern Singapore's founding in 1819, the Chinese community in Malacca represented one of the oldest concentrations of Chinese in maritime South East Asia. No doubt the first Chinese merchant-adventurers who came to Malacca in the 15th and 16th centuries expected to return to their native land one day — the ties of family and descent that bind one to one's ancestral home are a powerful force in traditional Chinese culture — but like so many of those who came after them, things just didn't work out that way and they stayed. Almost without exception

these early settlers would have been men and they naturally took themselves a wife and had children (even those who did eventually return to China usually entered into temporary marriages while living overseas — it was a recognised custom at the time). These wives were not Chinese wives; rather, they were local girls, probably not Muslim Malays but women from non-Muslim communities, originating in other parts of the Malay and Indonesian archipelagos. In time, the descendents of these unions between male Chinese settlers and local women gave rise to a kind of hybrid Sino-Malay culture, which though firmly rooted in Chinese traditions and beliefs, was acculturated by an overlay of local customs and practices, including the adoption of the Malay language, albeit in a rather bastardised form.

Similar stories of Chinese settlement, intermarriage and cultural assimilation (at least in part), were occurring all over maritime South East Asia from the 16th century onwards if not earlier. In the Malay and Indonesian archipelagos, these communities of assimilated Chinese

LEFT Interior of a Chinese merchant's house, Hoi Ann, Vietnam. Like Malacca, coastal Hoi An is another example of an ancient Chinese mercantile community, long settled in the region.

ABOVE Nineteenth-century painting of Chinese shophouses in Bangkok; note the traditional single-plank shutters that were inserted individually to close up the shop at night.

ABOVE RIGHT Traditional Chinese-style Malaccan townhouses in Jalan Tun Tan Cheng Lock (formerly Heeren Street). Their obvious correspondence with other Chinese houses found elsewhere in Nanyang, most notably Hoi An in Vietnam (see above) and Batavia, the former Dutch capital of the Netherlands East Indies, clearly indicates that these building represent a generic building type common to the region.

RIGHT Airwell in a Chinese merchant's house, Malacca, from the turn of the last century.

are generally referred to as Peranakan — the term derives from the

Malay word *anak*, meaning "child" and, in this context, signifies someone who is native born but who is not an indigene of the country.

The fidelity of these Peranakan Chinese communities to the customs of their ancestors, at least in terms of their dress and ritual observations, extended to the realm of architecture. It has often been noted that Chinese temples in South East Asia closely resemble those in southern China, and the same is true for domestic architecture, which is very similar to that of the southernmost coastal provinces of Guangdong and Fujian. Malacca, Batavia, Hoi Ann in Vietnam — wherever one goes there is a recognisable Nanyang-style Chinese house — and it is this same archetype which found its way to Singapore with the first wave of Chinese immigration to the island in the early 1820s.

# EARLY SINGAPORE

The early buildings of Singapore were constructed from local materials — mainly timber and attap thatch — but with the rapid

ABOVE  Surviving portion of Baba Yeo Kim Swee's godowns, photographed in the 1950s.

BELOW  Reconstruction of Baba Yeo Kim Swee's godowns, designed by George Coleman in 1841/1842. The arcaded walkway and warehouse space on the ground floor, with business premises or coolie accommodation above, established a precedent for subsequent commercial buildings in early 19th century Singapore.

development of Raffles' new trading post, it wasn't long before the pioneer settlers, both European and Chinese, began to build more permanent structures out of bricks and mortar with tiled roofs. Visual records for this period are limited, but in the case of those erected by the Chinese, it seems reasonable to suppose they were pretty much like contemporary Chinese buildings in Malacca and other Nanyang city-ports. While, the correspondences between this style of architecture and the Singapore shophouse are immediately apparent, they are not quite the same thing, and this is where Sir Stamford Raffles (1781–1826) and his advisor, the Irish architect and surveyor, George Drumgoolde Coleman, enter the story.

What Raffles brought to the table was his vision of the future Singapore as a grand metropolis, a modern city, a new "Venice of the East". Coleman, for his part, provided a neo-Classical backdrop for this vision. Working together, the two men came up with a town plan and urban architectural idiom that would more or less define the look of Singapore as a city, until the era of the skyscraper and shopping mall.

Raffles had a good idea of how he wanted Singapore to be right from the very start: On 4 November 1822, he issued a far-reaching set of Ordinances for the layout and future development of Singapore town with instructions that even went as far as the actual design and construction of the buildings themselves. Thus we find him advising his Town Committee: "To preserve uniformity and regularity hereafter, you will be pleased to class the streets

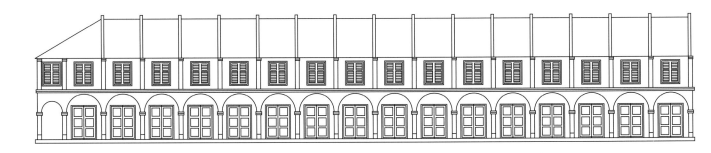

LEFT From the earliest days of settlement the Singapore River was the city's main artery of commerce and remained so until well into the 20th century.

BELOW LEFT Lithograph of the Singapore River, probably taken in the mid-1860s; Baba Yeo Kim Swee's godown can be seen on the north bank, just below the new Elgin Bridge, which was constructed in 1862.

BELOW RIGHT An engraving of Chinatown, taken in 1837, in which we clearly see the Chinese character of the early buildings erected along the south bank of the river (today's Boat Quay), with their distinctive "crawling cat" gables and tiled roofs.

according to the relative advantages of situation under the heads of 1st, 2nd, and 3rd class, determining the least space along the street which shall be occupied by each house and consequently fixing the exact number of houses which each street shall contain."

This, in effect, determined a standard size for each building on either side of a particular road, at least in terms of their street frontage, which was set at around 20 feet (7 m). The houses themselves were to be of brick and tile, a requirement that was intended, at least in part, to reduce the risks of large-scale conflagrations. To this Raffles added one more stipulation, namely that "for the sake of uniformity and gaining as much room as possible … a still further accommodation will be afforded to the public by requiring that each house should have a verandah of a certain depth, open at all times as a continued and covered passage on each side of the street."

Thus, the basic formula for the Singapore shophouse was established, and it only needed George Drumgoolde Coleman to determine how it should look. Coleman was Singapore's first and, for many years, only professionally trained architect. Before coming to Singapore he had previously practiced in Calcutta and Batavia, and thus had plenty of experience of designing for the tropics. But Coleman also came from a Classical background — he had been on the Grand Tour and was familiar with the colonnaded *piazzas* of 16th-century Italy as well as their reinvention in contemporary Regency architecture in England — and we see these influences at work in his warehouses along the river, which at once recall Renaissance prototypes while simultaneously establishing a precedent for the future development of the Singapore shophouse.

# THE EARLY SHOPHOUSE

By the mid-1840s the town of Singapore was rapidly expanding with new roads being laid out both to the north and south of the river. The principle area of expansion during this period was south of the river, between South Bridge and New Bridge roads — by the late 1840s, shophouse development had reached as far as Temple Street by this time, though there were still plenty of building plots which had yet to be taken up closer to the river.

The earliest permanent shophouses were fairly perfunctory structures: two storeys, with the upper floor projecting over the covered walkway beneath, supported by a pair of square-plan columns, which were carried through to the upper storey as pilasters. There was very little attempt at ornamentation to the façade: a rudimentary cornice, and a bit of moulding to serve as a capital for the columns and pilasters, and that was about it. The windows were square-headed with jalousie shutters — unlike

Coleman's godowns along the river there were two to a bay, that is to say, each shophouse unit. The arcaded verandah that we see in Coleman's godowns was omitted in favour of a simple wooden beam spanning the interval between the columns. Lastly, the roof was laid with clay tiles; the latter were manufactured locally, possibly to a Portuguese design (see page 80).

Relatively cheap in terms of labour and materials, this early style of shophouse, which was already in place around 1840, continued to be built in large numbers up until the 1870s and even later. There are still a few surviving examples in Chinatown, but most of the inner city was redeveloped and rebuilt at the turn of the last century.

An early visitor, Major James Low (later Lieutenant-Colonel) of the Madras Army, noted in his journal (*circa* 1840/1841): "The Chinese build their homes with brick and mortar when they can afford it, the Malays seldom or never.... The streets of the native town are spacious and they are crowded with native shops. A stranger may well amuse himself for a couple of hours in threading the piazzas in front of the shops, which he can do so unmolested by the sun, at any hour of the day." Clearly, the term *piazza*, as used here, is a reference to Raffles' five-foot way.

LEFT A street in Chinatown photographed in the 1880s, but the houses are probably a lot older and exemplify the mid-19th century Singapore shophouse — pragmatic but plain with jalousie windows but little by way of architectural embellishment or detailing. Courtesy of NAS.

RIGHT AND BELOW The Ellenborough Building in elevation and as it looked in the early 1950s. The Classical detailing may have been a bit heavy-handed, but it was a step in the right direction, as a correspondent in the *Singapore Free Press* in 1845, reporting on the progress of Singapore in that year, noted: "Tan Tock Seng is far advanced with erection of an extensive range of shops on a uniform plan and with more pretensions to architectural beauty that the general run of such boutiques."

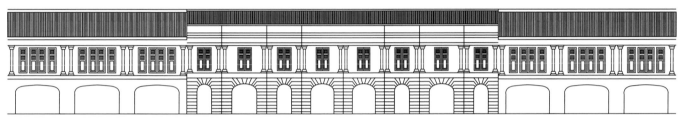

As well as being a period during which we see a rapid expansion of the town, the 1840s also witnessed an improvement in the quality of buildings being erected. A good example of this was the Ellenborough Building, named after Lord Ellenborough, Governor-General of India. Occupying a triangular site between Ellenborough Street, Boat Quay and Eu Tong Sen Street, the land had been acquired by a local worthy, Tan Tock Seng, for $7,000.

Malaccan-born, Tan was a self-made man who had started out with a fruit and vegetable stall but had invested his money wisely and by this time was fabulously wealthy. He was a philanthropist too, being the main sponsor of the Thian Hock Keng temple on Telok Ayer street as well as the prime instigator behind the building of a Paupers' Hospital on the slopes of Pearl Hill, which later came to be renamed after its principal benefactor.

As the architect of his new commercial venture, Tan Tock Seng commissioned Government Surveyor, John Turnbull Thomson, who had designed the hospital for him the previous year. Thomson, a

Scot, had come out East in 1838 as an employee of Scott & Co, Penang, but had taken up the post of Government Surveyor following Coleman's early death in 1841 — Thomson was only 20 at the time.

The building was a two-storey affair distinguished by an arcaded five-foot way in the manner of Coleman's riverside godowns from a few years earlier, except that where Coleman had employed semi-circular arches, Thompson opted for three-centred arches, which allowed for a slightly wider bay. Many of the units had a river frontage so they could be used as godowns for storing commodities awaiting transhipment or re-export. The corner units had a rusticated basement with a parapet rising above the roofline.

Ultimately, the Ellenborough Building may not have been the most elegant of edifices in terms of its proportions, but it was certainly a step in the right direction in terms of coming up with a more evolved facade for the Singapore shophouse.

# THE SECOND-GENERATION SHOPHOUSE

Although the mid-19th century shophouse was still fairly basic as far as architectural elements are concerned — architraves, cornices, pilasters and so forth — there is evidence of increasing decorative sophistication, most notably in terms of surface ornamentation and the quality of materials used, as the century progressed. One recalls François-Edmond Pâris' description of Singapore in 1831, where he mentions how the Chinese merchants "decorate their houses with bizarre taste which is typical of their nation", adding that "the façades are covered with brightly coloured frescoes". No doubt this tendency towards greater decorative elaboration went hand in hand with the increasing prosperity and viability of Singapore as a regional centre of trade and commerce.

The first generation of immigrants from China or Nanyang had not seen themselves as settlers per se; rather they were following the traditional Chinese practice of sojourning, intending to return home at a later date. Come the 1860s and '70s, there was a growing tendency among older Chinese residents — those who had made some money and were doing well in their business ventures — to make Singapore their permanent home. With this in mind, they sent to China for their wives and other family members; and they also began to build more substantial homes for themselves — no doubt a certain amount of ostentation and rivalry played its part here.

LEFT  Chinese-ornamented shophouse in Smith Street with an interlocking swastika pattern incised in the plasterwork. In Buddhist iconography, the swastika signifies eternality and represents the *Dharma*, or Buddhist way, as based on the teachings of the Gautama Buddha; the Chinese thought it also had a talismanic quality to ward of evil influences.

The characteristic feature of this second-generation Singapore shophouse would seem to have been a proliferation of surface ornamentation mainly in the form of stucco reliefs and decorative panels. The motifs seem to have been almost wholly Chinese in inspiration and they went hand in hand with an ensemble of other traditional Chinese structural decorative elements which included granite lintels and thresholds; sculpted wooden beams and corbels, the details picked out in gold leaf; latticework screens and elaborately carved door and window panels; *chien nien* mosaic reliefs and painted plaques; green-glazed airbricks and ceramic bamboo-style window mullions. Canopy roofs, resting on granite brackets projecting over the five-foot way, were another Chinese feature that became popular as the century progressed. In this instance the tiles were imported from China (as opposed to

ABOVE Although there are very few remaining examples of a Chinese-style shophouse left intact, the Baba House on Neil Road being a notable exception (see pages 98–101), Chinese decorative elements survive in great profusion. Here, we see a collection of scrolls, *chien nien* work, calligraphy and more, many from houses on Stanley Street.

the v-shaped tiles of local manufacture which were used for the main roof), with green-glazed stoppers or end-pieces for the roof margins, which had a drip tip to aid the run off of rain water.

All of these elements had become a standard part of the shophouse repertoire by the last decade of the 19th century and they continued to be popular well into the next. Together, they constitute what might be described as the Chinese-style shophouse since the influences are almost wholly Chinese in origin, the jalousie windows and open-plan five-foot way aside.

# SINGAPORE'S COURTYARD HOUSES

Associated with Singapore's growing prosperity towards the end of the 19th century, one begins to find an increasing number of wealthy Chinese merchants or *towkays*, who began to build homes of varying degrees of extravagance for themselves. Some were inclined to follow the precedent set by one Hoo Ah Kay, better known as Whampoa, the first Chinese member of the colonial administration's Legislative Council, who built himself a European-style mansion on the outskirts of town in the 1840s. There were others, though, who preferred to follow in the footsteps of their ancestors by opting for a traditional courtyard house. Despite being so far from home and surrounded by barbarians, the idea still proved irresistible for those who could afford it.

In all, no more than about half a dozen of these buildings were erected in Singapore and, sadly, only two have survived to this day. Both belonged to Towkay Tan Yeok Nee, a successful pepper and gambier planter in Johor, who subsequently became a partner with Tan Seng Poh in the lucrative opium and spirit farms in Singapore, as well as a major property owner with a string of shophouses and commercial premises along the river. One of his homes stands at the junction of Clemenceau Avenue and Penang Road; built in 1882, it is now home to the Chicago Business School. The other is on Clarke Quay and is currently a restaurant and club.

Both these residences are in the style of a southern Chinese courtyard house, being symmetrical in plan, about a longitudinal axis, with the ancestral hall at the centre and courtyards front and back, as well as suites of rooms on either side. They were very richly ornamented using traditional materials imported from China.

Chinese master builders and craftsmen had of course been present in the region since the earliest of time, their skills and technical knowledge sought after for the construction of temples, medical halls, clan houses and other prestige buildings; now,

ABOVE  Portrait of Tan Yeok Nee. Courtesy of NAS.

OPPOSITE TOP  Entrance pavilion — the upturned swallow tail roof ridge is a characteristic feature of southern Chinese architecture in Guangdong province, from where Yeok Nee originally hailed.

OPPOSITE MIDDLE LEFT  Stuccowork of lucky pomegranates on a side wall.

OPPOSITE MIDDLE RIGHT  The rear of the two-storey wing, which was where the bedrooms were situated, opens onto a secluded courtyard.

OPPOSITE BOTTOM  Open-air corridors and passageways connect the main pavilions within the domestic compound.

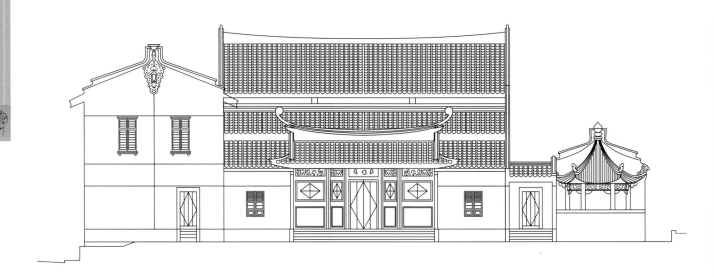

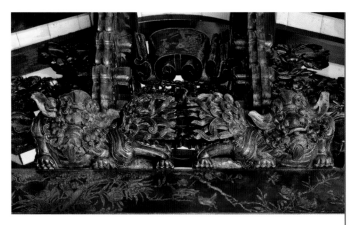

ABOVE  Front elevation of Tan Yeok Nee Mansion, with the roof of the ancestral hall rising above the roofs of other less prestigious structures in the domestic compound.

LEFT  The eaves of the main hall are supported on the back of a pair of magnificent Chinese lions, symbolising power and protection.

OPPOSITE TOP  The roof of the main hall is supported by traditional bracket and beam timber framework. In Singapore this kind of roof is usually only found in temples, clan associations and other prestige buildings; only the very wealthy could afford to build their homes in such a manner.

OPPOSITE BOTTOM LEFT  Decorative stucco panel from the entrance porch.

OPPOSITE BOTTOM RIGHT  Decorative fish. The fish is a symbol of wealth in traditional Chinese iconography, the term for "fish" and "abundance" being pronounced the same way (*yu*). Fish also symbolise harmony, marital happiness and plenty of children, because they sometimes swim in pairs and multiply rapidly. Sadly, by the time of his death in China (where he had another huge mansion) in 1902, Tan Yeok Nee's sons had all predeceased him.

with the growing prosperity of Singapore as a Crown Colony, they found themselves called upon to apply their talents to residential architecture.

As far as the evolution of the shophouse is concerned, the point about the *towkays* and their courtyard houses is that they seem to have ushered in a kind of Chinese renaissance in Singapore — a renewed interest or enthusiasm in the arts and crafts of their homeland. Perhaps it had never really gone away, but with the increasing prosperity of Singapore, and a growing sense of security in terms of the settlement's status as a permanent feature on the map of South East Asia, the better-off felt more inclined to invest their money in things of beauty and permanence — and this included their homes. Thus, in the last couple of decades of the 19th century, we see an increasing use of traditional Chinese decorative motifs and the ornamentation of the shophouse façade, as well as their interiors.

# TOWKAYS AND TOWNHOUSES

Only the very rich could afford to build a courtyard house downtown — the price of land near the centre was pretty steep even at this moment in time and a courtyard house required three or four adjacent parcels of land. However, there was plenty of scope for taking the basic shophouse formula and developing it into a more imposing kind of residence by simply adding an extra storey and enhancing the façade with an assortment of traditional Chinese decorative embellishments.

No better example of a *towkay*'s townhouse at the turn of the last century exists than the Baba House in Neil Road (the term "Baba' was used to refer to Peranakan Chinese of Malacca origin, many of whom were among the first to come to Singapore in the early days of settlement). Evidence suggests that the building was designed by the Almeida & Kassim partnership who made something of a speciality out of designing Chinese-style houses for rich *towkays*. Certainly, the Baba House bears all the hallmarks of their work, including an ornately carved entrance door with a *pintu pagar* (saloon-style door) and scrolls over the ground floor windows; a canopy roof surmounted by *chien nien* frieze; stucco panels with traditional scenes in relief, plus added colour; and ornate shutters with Chinese designs surmounted by panels with auspicious characters in *chien nien* mosaics. The upper storey was added later, as evidenced by the Georgian-style fanlights above the windows, slightly out of character with the rest of the facade.

Conceptually the ground floor plan of the Baba House is identical to that of a traditional courtyard house, with the skywell taking on the role of the courtyard. In this scheme of things, the front room fulfills the same function as the main hall for receiving

ABOVE The internal skywell with the family altar, dedicated to the ancestors, visible along the back wall of the rear pavilion. This was the main living "room" of the house, a cool and tranquil retreat from the hustle and bustle of town.

OPPOSITE The richly ornamented front of the house, with its *chien nien* frieze, Chinese-tile canopy roof, gilded brackets and intricately carved *pintu pagar*, representing the very best of traditional Chinese craftsmanship and materials. The characters on the board over the top of the door read "The Glory of the Lineage" (*zhong sheng*). Interestingly, despite being set back from the road, the entrance to the house is still modelled on that of a shophouse, with a five-foot way style verandah.

visitors in a courtyard house. The principal focal point is an altar dedicated to the household deity, Guan Gong, the Chinese god of war, who is renowned for his courage, loyalty and righteousness. This is placed at the far end, directly facing the front door to ward off any evil influences that might attempt to cross the threshold, and the rest of the room is symmetrically arranged around this central axis. An intricately carved latticework screen overlaid with gold leaf separates the front room from the family apartments behind; only close relatives and the most intimate of family friends would be invited beyond this point. The principal living area within the Baba House is arranged around the internal courtyard or skywell, the Chinese equivalent of the Englishman's verandah, with ornamental plants in hand-painted ceramic bowls sitting atop glazed jardinières. This was where family meals were eaten and the occupants of the house relaxed during their leisure hours, playing cards or *mah jong*. The natural ventilation, created by the airwell, made this a cool and restful place to sit, even in the hottest of weathers.

A second altar, along the rear wall of the family hall, is dedicated to the family ancestors — this occupies an analogous position to the ancestral hall, or *zhengwu*, in a traditional courtyard house. The wooden ancestral tablets recording the names and achievements of past family members were housed in a special cabinet whose carved panels depict scenes of filial piety. Beyond the family hall, lay the kitchen area, with laundry facilities as well as a bathroom and privy at the very rear of the house. In Peranakan homes where the preparation and consumption of food had an almost ritualistic dimension to it, the kitchen area was one of the most important spaces in the house, being referred to metaphorically as the *perut rumah* or "stomach of the house". As the authors of *Rumah Baba: Life in a Peranakan House* observe: "In the days when young ladies had no access to formal education, culinary skills were among the chief accomplishments necessary for a well brought-up Nonya [and] cooking became a very intricate and complicated art" (the term "Nonya" was the feminine counterpart of Baba.)

The floor above was given over to bedrooms and this being a Peranakan house, special emphasis was placed on the bridal chamber which was situated at the front of the house, directly over the reception hall (see opposite top).

ABOVE  Decorative plaster panel at the foot of the staircase, depicting paired phoenixes with a peony, signifying lovers and connubial intercourse. Decorative plaque in the form of a scroll, from the entrance porch. The characters refer to the purple-flowered "orchid tree" (*Bauhinia* spp), which in Chinese iconography represents harmony within the household.

OPPOSITE TOP  The bridal suite, which is situated on the first floor directly over the reception hall. Since the Baba House was home to a Peranakan family, no expense was spared in the decoration of the bridal bed and chamber (see fabric below).

OPPOSITE BOTTOM LEFT  The front reception room on the ground floor, which is dominated at the far end by an ornate screen and in front of it, a shrine dedicated to the house deity, in this instance the warrior god, Guan Gong, or Guan Yu.

OPPOSITE BOTTOM RIGHT  As was usually the case in long-established Peranakan families who had close dealings with the British, the furniture and ornaments reflect an eclectic mix of European and Chinese aesthetic sensibilities.

# A CLASSICAL EDUCATION

What has come to be known as the "Chinese Baroque shophouse", a style that flourished between 1895 and 1905, represents one of the high water marks of shophouse architecture. Classical influences had been there right from the start, of course, notably in George Coleman's godown architecture and prestige projects like John Turnbull Thomson's Ellenborough Building (see page 91), but it is not until the late 1880s that we see a conscious attempt to develop a Classically-inspired language for the shophouse façade.

It has been suggested that the crossover was a fairly haphazard affair with local Asian builders more or less randomly appropriating Classical features from the colonial architecture that they saw around them. For example, architectural historian, Lee Kip Lin, writes of the "untutored ... application of classical features", in a manner that was "spontaneous, unsophisticated and hybrid", and there is truth in what he says. However, at the same time the process of adoption, especially in the initial stages, was rather more measured than that, not least because it was European architects who were the first to introduce Classical elements into the shop-house repertoire in a logical and coherent manner.

We can be fairly certain about this because it is in the mid 1880s that the architectural records kick in, with the earliest submission of working drawings to the Municipality for planning permission dating from 1884. After this point, one can be much more precise about the advent of particular architectural features and styles, and who was responsible for their introduction, whether in relation to shophouses, or any other kind of building for that matter.

Possibly the very first instance of a Classically-influenced shophouse façade — certainly the earliest on record — dates from 1886, namely a row of four three-storey shophouses in Sago Street designed by Henry Richard for a client by the name of Lee Ah Tok. Richard was a former Overseer of Public Works and Discipline Officer of Convicts in the Public Works Department, but seems to have gone into private practice as an architect around 1885. Although his background is unknown, Richard clearly had some kind of formal architectural training as his godown on D'Almeida Street in 1886 evinces (see left). Here we see a well organised

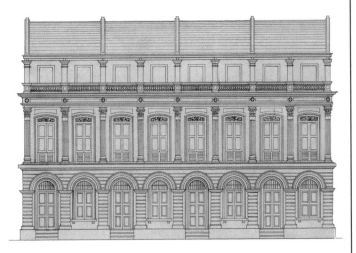

ABOVE Godown for Tan Chin Hoon at D'Almeida Street, Henry Richard, 1886. Although this building was ostensibly designed as a warehouse, with storage on the ground floor, and business premises and clerical workspace above, it clearly lends itself to reinterpretation in a shophouse context. Richard designed a number of godowns like this in the business district in the early-to-mid 1880s and it was perhaps inevitable that he should draw on the same basic material when he came to his shophouses in Sago Street, which were designed just a couple of months after this building (see page 105). BCA Collection, courtesy of NAS.

OPPOSITE Three shophouses at Duxton Hill for Tham Hee Foon by Lermit & Westerhout, 1902. The partnership of Alfred Lermit and Josiah Westerhout were major players in the development of the Classical shophouse façade around the turn of the last century. The Chinese-style canopy roof aside, the façade of these buildings is almost wholly European in inspiration with their fluted Corinthian pilasters and dentiled cornices.

Classical façade with a rusticated podium, or basement, at street level and Ionic pilasters dividing the window bays above; the upper storey is set back to create a modest terrace with a parapet of green-glazed balusters.

The D'Almeida Street drawings were submitted for planning permission in July 1886 and just a few weeks later he submitted his application for Ah Tok's shophouses on Sago Street. The elevations are not as detailed as the D'Almeida Street godown, but the application of Classical orders is perfectly correct in terms of its accordance with Roman preferences: Doric piers at the ground floor level, Ionic pilasters for the floor above and Corinthian pilasters for the upper storey. There are no secondary pilasters or fancy architraves and the cornice is relatively simple, but there are Georgian fanlights over the first floor windows. Indeed, the terrace would not have looked out of place in either Cheltenham or Bath (two English spa towns celebrated for their fine Georgian architecture).

Once it was in place, this basic configuration was rapidly developed and elaborated upon by local Singaporean architects, and within a decade we see the emergence of mature, Classically-inspired, turn-of-the-century shophouse rows that still line the streets of Chinatown today, particularly in the Kreta Ayer district. Like the Baroque masters of the 16th and 17th centuries, local builders and architects took the basic ingredients of the Classical idiom, which they had learnt from their mentors — most Singaporean architects in the 19th and early 20th centuries started out as draughtsmen in the Public Works Department or working for European architectural practices — and reinvented them to suit their own needs and purposes.

The end result was a very singular style of architecture. Though it made use of Classical elements, and even followed some of the rules of Classical architecture in terms of their application, it was not

in the strictest sense of the term Classical architecture. Certainly there is nothing like the Singapore shophouse in Rome or Florence or anywhere else in the world for that matter, except in the region round about. However, the spirit of inventiveness, the richness of ornamentation and playful reinterpretation of the Classical idiom, is quintessentially Baroque, and it seems reasonable, therefore, to refer to this style of architecture as "Chinese Baroque", as indeed others have done in the past. However, some qualification is necessary here, for while it is true that many of the leading exponents of this style were indeed Chinese, it was not the sole preserve of Chinese architects and one comes across a number of Eurasian, Indian, Malay and even English architects who were equally adept at working in this idiom.

OPPOSITE  Singaporean Baroque at the turn of the last century: shophouses like these lined both sides of Tanjong Pagar Road (top) creating an imposing introduction to Singapore as one proceeded from the docks at Keppel harbour towards the centre of town. Similar buildings in Mohamed Sultan Road (below) are actually "dwelling houses", the former homes of Singapore's rich *towkay* families, who, beginning in the 1890s, began to abandon Chinatown for more salubrious locations in the surrounding hills.

ABOVE  These shophouses in Sago Street, designed by Henry Richard for Lee Ah Tok in 1886, would seem to be the earliest instance of a properly-considered, Classically-inspired shophouse façade, especially in relation to the correct application of Classical of orders — Doric at the bottom, Ionic above and Corinthian on top.

RIGHT  Baroque townhouses at Mohamed Sultan Road from the turn of the last century.

# LOCAL HEROES:
## THE BAROQUE MASTERS

British architects may have been the first to introduce Classical elements into the shophouse repertoire, but it was local Singaporean

architects who were largely responsible for coming up with the fully mature, Classically-inspired shophouse façade of the late-1890s. The key figures here are the Chinese triumvirate of Wee Teck Moh, Loh Kiam Siew and Yeo Hock Siang, Malay architect Wan Mohamed Kassim, and George d'Almeida, who was of Portuguese descent. Not a great deal is known about the lives of any of these men, their names coming down to us as fading signatures on yellowing working drawings deposited with the National Archives. But they are the unsung heroes of Singapore architecture and we see evidence of their achievements about us every day as we walk through Chinatown or take a stroll up Emerald Hill.

It was these architects that were responsible for the sudden explosion of creative energy that took the relatively straightforward Richard-style shophouse façade and turned it into a Baroque extravaganza that would have raised a few eyebrows even in 17th-century Rome. Up until this time, most shophouse designers had opted for the Doric order, with its no-nonsense capitals and relatively simple entablature, the one exception being Richard himself who favoured the Ionic order with its curling ram-horn capitals. Midway through the 1890s, however, Corinthian — with its fluted pilasters, leafy capitals and richly ornamented cornices complete with dentils and egg and dart mouldings — becomes very much the order of the day. It is this highly ornate style that has come to define the Chinese Baroque shophouse.

LEFT  Two dwelling houses for Messrs Lee Hong & Chun Seng Lin at Club Street, Hock Siang & Kiam Siew, 1896. While European architects may have been the first to consider a Classically-conceived shophouse façade, it was local architects like Yeo Hock Siang and his partner Loh Kiam Siew, who developed the idea and came up with the fully mature Singapore Baroque style; these paired townhouses on Club Street are an early instance of this. BCA Collection, courtesy of NAS.

The other important stylistic development was the introduction of the secondary pilaster to divide the windows into separate and clearly-defined bays, the arch of the window itself — rounded headed or segmental — springing from their capital. The inspiration, here, almost certainly came from the big commercial buildings along the water front and around Raffles Place which were designed by European architects.

It is the combination of the secondary pilaster, augmented by Corinthian order, which gives us the mature Baroque shophouse façade in all its glory. The first time we see this is in 1896 when a certain Chong Yip & Co commissioned the rebuilding of six three-storey shophouse units on the corner of Smith and Trengganu Streets (below). The architects were Yeo Hock Siang, who had trained as a draughtsman under Henry Richard, and Loh Kiam Siew, who styled themselves as Hock Siang & Kiam Siew. The order is Corinthian from top to bottom with a denticulated cornice, as appropriate, Regency fanlights with keystones, and relief work filling in the spandrels — the full Monty in other words.

ABOVE Townhouse, Club Street, Hock Siang & Kiam Siew, 1896.

LEFT The rebuilding of six shophouses, on the corner of Smith Street and Trengganu Street from 1896, seems a likely candidate for the very first instance in which we see the fully-realised Chinese Baroque shophouse, complete with secondary pilasters, Corinthian capitals and cornices, and Regency fanlights. Again, it was Messrs Hock Siang and Kiam Siew who came up with the idea for Chong Yip & Co. Remarkably, the building is still with us, more or less unchanged, to this day.

If Yeo Hock Siang was the originator of the fully-realised Baroque shophouse, it wasn't long before other architectural practices took up the style, most notably Wee Teck Moh (see overleaf) and the practice of Almeida & Kassim.

George d'Almeida, the gransdson of famous Singapore pioneer Portuguese physician Dr José d'Almeida, had started out as a surveyor with the Public Works Department in Malacca, while Wan Mohamad Kassim, a Malay architect, had previously been with Henry Richard as his clerk of works. Their combined talents put them at the forefront of shophouse design for the duration of their partnership (1895–1901), and also after they had gone their separate ways. Initially successful as the purveyors of finely crafted

ABOVE These two townhouses in Club Street, which date from 1897, represent an interesting point of transition between Almeida & Kassim's "*towkay* townhouse style" and the Baroque blockbuster which was just at that very moment about to erupt on the scene.

MIDDLE Much of the Kreta Ayer district of Chinatown was rebuilt around the turn of the last century, the old two-storey mid-19th century shophouses being replaced by modern, magisterial three-storey Baroque numbers. Large chunks of Mosque Street (shown here) were redeveloped between 1900 and 1901 and most of the work was carried out by the practice of Almeida & Kassim; note the employment of pedimented secondary pilasters.

Chinese-style townhouses — the Baba House is most likely one of their designs — they were no less adept in their handling of the Classical idiom. One particular innovation of theirs was the pedimented secondary pilaster, which is a very curious and, I might add, uniquely Singaporean feature, but one that rapidly became an integral part of the standard Baroque shophouse repertoire. In some instances, the secondary pilaster, instead of supporting the arch of the window head like it was supposed to do, became an entirely independent structure in its own right. It still divided the shophouse façade into bays, but no longer had any logical connection to the windows in a structural sense.

RIGHT TOP Window glazing came in at around the time of the Baroque revolution. It was preceded by glazed fanlights, before proceeding to the shutters themselves, though at first it was only the well-to-do who could afford this innovation.

RIGHT MIDDLE Pedimented window heads, instead of fanlights or ventilation grilles, were not that common but there is nice example on Duxton Road, from the drawing board of George d'Almeida, in 1902 — d'Almeida was now practicing on his own, the partnership with Wan Mohamad Kassim having been dissolved the previous year.

RIGHT BOTTOM The pedimented secondary pilaster just before it broke loose from the window altogether.

# WEE TECK MOH:
## SHOPHOUSE KING

If Yeo Hock Siang can be seen as the originator of the classic Baroque shophouse façade, then Wee Teck Moh was surely the grandmaster.

Again, we know frustratingly little about him in terms of his life and who he was, but it is the genius of Wee Teck Moh that defines the classic turn-of-the century shophouse in its most elevated form.

Wee Teck Moh drifts into the picture in 1890 with the re-building of a modest two-storey shophouse on Duxton Hill — one of the very earliest to be built there. On the working drawings, Wee Teck Moh politely identifies himself as "drauftsman" [sic], which gives us a clue to his possible origins in the architectural department of an engineering firm or land auctioneer company. A few months later he has entered into partnership with Wan Mohamad Kassim. Most of the work of this short-lived practice was fairly perfunctory, but a couple of early commissions reveal the influence of Kassim's former mentor, Henry Richard.

By the beginning of 1892, Wee Teck Moh struck out on his own, which was the way it was to stay for the rest of his career. He took a while to get into his stride, though, and it is not until we get to a couple of townhouses on Club Street, in 1894, with ornate, Chinese-influenced interiors, that we see Wee Teck Moh beginning to realise his talents as an architect. More townhouses followed, but in 1897 we encounter the first examples of his mature shophouse style — Corinthian pilasters and comices, Regency-style fanlights, *chien nien* friezes and a lot of twiddly bits in between.

No doubt the work of his contemporaries — Yeo Hock Siang, and the partnership of George d'Almeida and Wan Mohamad Kassim — played some part in Wee Teck Moh's development, in that they began designing shophouses in the Baroque style a year or so before he got in on the act. Once started, though, Wee Teck Moh was quick to make it his own and, as time went by, he gradually refined the style in terms of proportions and the articulation of individual elements. By 1903, he had taken the Sino-Baroque shophouse to its ultimate limits, his townhouse for the Seah family on Emerald Hill being perhaps the most sublime example of his art still standing.

OPPOSITE The subtle play of light on the façade of 90 Amoy Street, brings to life all the intricacy of Wee Teck Moh's creative skills.

ABOVE Wee Teck Moh reaches his apotheosis at 45 Emerald Hill, which he designed for the "Messrs Seah" in 1903 — Seah Boon Kang, and his brother Seah Boon Kiat, were the grandsons of wealthy Teochew pioneer, Seah Eu Chin, and they had bought the Emerald Hill estate some three years previously. Fronted by a traditional Chinese-gateway in the Teochew style, with *chien nien* frieze and upturned swallow tail roof ridge, the elegant Classical façade behind represents Singapore Baroque at its best.

RIGHT More Wee Teck Moh at Emerald Hill. Wee Teck Moh was responsible for more than a dozen houses along this street; this townhouse from 1903 features his vine motif, which was a recurrent decorative feature in his later work.

# THE MOVE TO
## HIGHER GROUND

By the early 1890s, Chinatown was becoming seriously overcrowded as each year brought ever-increasing numbers of skilled and unskilled Chinese immigrant labourers to Singapore. Shophouses that had once been home to family businesses were subdivided into cubicles to house the soaring numbers of urban poor, but there was no proper sanitation or sewerage, night-soil collection was inefficient and the water table polluted; Chinatown was becoming a very unhealthy and disagreeable place to live.

ABOVE Dwelling house at Mohamed Sultan Road for Ong Kee Soon Esq, Wee Teck Moh, 1900. Wee Teck Moh was the architect of choice for Singapore's affluent Peranakan and Straits Chinese merchants at the turn of the last century. BCA Collection, courtesy of NAS.

Up until this moment in time, the typical Chinese Singapore merchant, wealthy or poor, had lived over his business, as was the tradition in China; now, those who could afforded it started to move out of the centre of town to more salubrious areas. Wealthy *towkays* had long maintained a house in the country, so to speak, but at this point we see a more suburban kind of development comprising streets of townhouses rather than villas standing in their own grounds. In the parlance of the day, these terraces of purely residential units were described as "dwelling houses" to distinguish them from shophouses where the ground floor was given over to commercial activities, and also from landed properties or villas which were generally described as "compound houses".

In this period, the mid 1890s, we see what might be characterised as the move to higher ground. Club Street and Ann Siang Hill were the first to be developed, having up until this point survived as a kind of green island in the middle of Chinatown. Duxton Hill and Neil Road soon followed, along with Campong Martin and Mohamed Sultan Road, which ran round the bottom of Institution Hill. They were the very earliest Chinese residential suburbs and it is not until the beginning of the new century that the first townhouses were built on Emerald Hill and Mount Sophia.

The leading townhouse architects of this golden era included Almeida & Kassim, Yeo Hock Siang and Loh Kiam Siew, but at the turn of the century the most prolific townhouse architect was without doubt Wee Teck Moh, who at that moment was reaching the peak of his output in what was an extremely busy career. Club Street, Duxton Hill, Mohamed Sultan Road, River Valley Road, Emerald Hill, Prinsep Street — the energetic Wee Teck Moh was just about everywhere, it seems, busily building homes for members of Singapore's Chinese elite.

ABOVE  Mohamed Sultan Road (pictured) and the streets round about — River Valley Road, Tong Watt Road and Kim Yam Road — began to take off as a residential district in the early 1890s. Previously, there had been one or two country houses in the area standing in large grounds, but beginning in 1892, we see the first quality townhouses going up along Mohamed Sultan Road, a process which was continued into the early years of the next century.

# EMERALD HILL

The origins of Emerald Hill lie in the exodus of wealthy Chinese merchants and their families from Chinatown in the last decade of the 19th century, into the surrounding low-lying hills — many of them former nutmeg plantations — from where they looked down on Singapore rather in the same way that the suburbs of Hampstead and Highgate look down upon the city of London. Emerald Hill was a largely Peranakan enclave, the most famous former resident being Dr Lim Boon Keng — educationalist, polymath, philanthropist and much else besides — who lived at No 2.

The earliest houses in the street date from 1902 and development continued in a piecemeal fashion until the mid 1920s, but it has to be said that the best of the crop were built before World War 1, several of which were designed by Shophouse King, Wee Teck Moh. Combining European Classicism with Chinese decoration and symbolism in an eclectic synthesis of Eastern and Western architectural traditions, the oldest surviving townhouses on Emerald Hill, as depicted here, represent the architectural apogee of the Chinese Baroque period.

ABOVE AND RIGHT  For all the renovations, conversions and refurbishments of the past two decades, Emerald Hill still retains its historic flavour, a little bit of old China set down in the heart of modern Singapore.

OPPOSITE  Emerald Hill's reputation as an exclusive residential neighbourhood for Singapore's Peranakan elite in the first two decades of the last century is reflected in the quality of its architecture: tall Baroque townhouses set back from the street, most of them designed by the leading architects of the day — Wee Teck Moh, George d'Almeida, Wan Mohamad Kassim, and J B Westerhout among them.

190428 (Tallman)

# JUBILEE STYLE

Chinese Baroque may represent the high-water mark of the Classically inspired shophouse, but for a brief period at the turn of the last

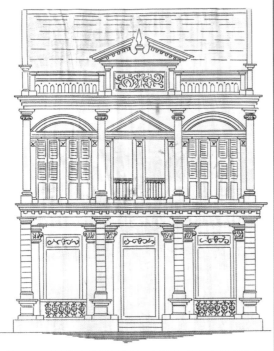

century it shared the limelight with a second *fin de siècle* shophouse style that started out from the same initial sources of inspiration but ended up in a rather different place. The latter style flourished for only a brief period — no more than about five years or so on the cusp of the century — and regrettably there are very few examples still surviving.

The underlying influences were again Baroque, but in this instance a Baroque style of Piranesian proportions — Giovanni Battista Piranesi was an 18th-century Italian artist, famous for his rather fantastical depictions of Classical ruins, where everything was slightly exaggerated or otherwise intensified to create a kind of epic quality or heightened sense of grandeur. Where the Singapore shophouse is concerned, the feeling is more monumental in character: the elevations are more extravagant, given over to grandiloquent gestures involving pediments and cartouches and other rhetorical flourishes. There is a greater degree of tension between the different elements in terms of their scale and mass; the facades are more sculptural, in the round, three-dimensional; the shadows deeper.

George d'Almeida and Wan Mohamad Kassim were without doubt the leading exponents of this alternative Baroque style, which developed out of their earlier work in the years leading up to the end of the century. In a five-year period between 1897 and 1902, which is when they went their separate ways, in addition to their Chinese-style townhouses for rich *towkays* and their more conventional turn-of-the century Baroque terraces, they also produced an astonishing range of highly original and sometimes quite exceptional Piranesian-style shophouses.

To a certain extent, the exuberance of Almeida & Kassim can be seen in a wider context as part of a more general outpouring of confidence and enthusiasm that preceded the run up to Queen Victoria's Diamond Jubilee in 1897 and continued through until her death four years later. This was a good time for Singapore and it is reflected in the architecture of the period. Significantly, many of

Almeida & Kassim's clients were wealthy Muslims of either Arab or Indian extraction — no doubt Kassim's own Muslim background played a part in securing their patronage. Both these communities had prospered under the British flag — prominent Arab families like the Alkaffs and Alsagoffs were major landowners and shipping magnates, while Indian Muslims were primarily engaged in business ventures and trade — and it seems that the more successful of them were keen to leave some kind of lasting impression on the urban landscape — in this particular instance, a terrace of shophouses conceived in the manner of a 17th-century Italian *palazzo*, or nobleman's palace, albeit on a somewhat reduced scale.

Set against this background, the architecture of Almeida & Kassim can be seen as a concrete realisation of the spirit of the age, a reflection of the imperial *zeitgeist*, celebrating what was in effect the zenith of the British Empire, though of course no one knew this at the time. In the circumstances, then, it seems appropriate to describe this particular style of shophouse architecture as the Jubilee style, a term that refers both to the period in which it was produced and to the nature of the architecture itself.

**OPPOSITE TOP** Almeida & Kassim townhouse at Sambawa Road (today's Beach Road Gardens), 1900. Each of the Almeida & Kassim shophouse facades from this period shows every sign of having been carefully thought out on its own merits and no two shophouses are alike. There is always some embellishment or slightly different arrangement of elements to ensure that each of their commissions was unique. BCA Collection, courtesy of NAS.

**OPPOSITE BOTTOM** One of a pair of surviving townhouses on Race Course Road, dating from 1902. Robust and forthright, they encapsulate the confidence of the late Victoria/early Edwardian era.

**ABOVE LEFT** Townhouse in Desker Road designed by Wan Mohamad Kassim in 1903. The working drawings identify the client as being one "W M Kassim", which suggests that the house may have been intended as Kassim's own residence; either that, or it was a shrewd investment property, in what was then an up and coming neighbourhood.

**ABOVE RIGHT** Rustication, cartouches, ornamental urns, and, in this instance, even a Saracenic onion dome, were all part of the decorative repertoire of the Jubilee style.

# THE EDWARDIAN SHOPHOUSE

The Jubilee style was relatively short lived, being extremely popular for four or five years around the turn of the last century, after which it went into decline. It can, however, be seen as an epiphenomenon of a more widespread revival of enthusiasm for Classical architecture in the late Victorian times, which eventually morphed into the Edwardian Baroque style of the early 20th century — R A J Bidwell's Victoria Memorial Hall and the contemporaneous refurbishment of Empress Place are the best example of this. Where the Singapore shophouse is concerned, the style is associated more with the work of British architects and engineers, familiar with the latest architectural fashions and stylistic developments in England, than their Asian counterparts.

At the turn of the century, there were two major British architectural practices on the scene, namely Swan & Maclaren and Lermit & Westerhout. Former surveyor turned architect, Alfred Lermit (1850–1929) and the Dutch Eurasian Josiah Bartholomew Westerhout (1871–1937) were in partnership between 1897 and 1904. Although they all shared the same Classically-inspired background, the typical Lermit & Westerhout shophouse was a lot less "busy" than its Chinese counterpart, with a greater degree of circumspection in the handling of Classical elements and the correct use of orders; even the most modest Lermit & Westerhout shophouse was distinguished by a quiet elegance that is instantly recognisable. Characteristic features included a fondness for segmental arches with keystones for their window heads, Corinthian pilasters rising though two storeys, and roofline parapets with antefixes, urns and ornamental balls placed at strategic intervals.

The firm of Swan & Maclaren was established in 1892 by engineers, Archibald Swan and James William Boyd Maclaren, formerly with the Singapore Tramways Board. By the turn of the century, however, the role of leading man at Swan & Maclaren had passed to one Regent Alfred John Bidwell, who had joined the firm in 1895. Bidwell was a professionally trained architect — a former secretary of the prestigious Architectural Association in London no less — and a man of considerable ability who in his time was responsible for a number of major buildings in Singapore including

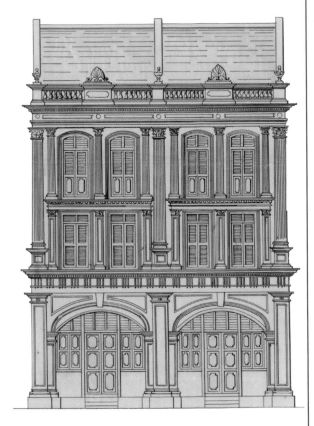

ABOVE  Two shophouses on Anson Road by Lermit & Westerhout for the estate of the late comprador, labour contractor and landed proprietor, Gan Eng Seng, from 1901. One intuitively senses a different kind of aesthetic at work here when compared to the more Baroque extravagances of their Chinese contemporaries. An interesting and uncommon feature is the use of a Doric frieze to divide the ground floor from the storey above. Note also the signature use of urns and antefixes along the top of the parapet at the roofline. BCA Collection, courtesy of NAS.

the rebuilding of Raffles Hotel (1899), the Teutonia Club (today's Goodwood Park Hotel) (1900), the Chased-El Synagogue (1905), the Victoria Memorial Hall (1905) and the Singapore Cricket Club (1907). Obviously, a man of Bidwell's talents was usually allocated the most prestigious commissions, but he did occasionally turn his hand to shophouse-style architecture, which is how he came to design the Eu Yan Sang pharmacy on South Bridge Road in 1910. It is an imposing, three-storey building in Bidwell's best Renaissance manner distinguished by an elegant loggia of Corinthian columns at the first floor level and a rather curious parapet wall at roof level, which seems to comprise Moorish elements, a not uncommon, if slightly eccentric, flourish found in a number of Bidwell's works.

TOP  Tropical Renaissance — the Eu Yan Sang Medical Hall on South Bridge Road, designed by Regent Alfred John Bidwell in 1910.

ABOVE  The only other Bidwell building in Chinatown is the magnificent Lai Chun Yuen Opera House on the corner of Smith and Trengganu streets. Although it was

designed in 1897, the opera house properly belongs to the Edwardian era in its restrained Classicism. An unusual feature, though, is the cantilevered wooden balcony running round the outside of the building at the second-storey level, which is something of a one-off in the shophouse repertoire.

# A NEW SHOPHOUSE
# CONFIGURATION

By the end of the 19th century, Chinatown was a disaster in the making. Years of continuously high levels of immigration from China had resulted in chronic overcrowding, which, compounded by poor sanitation, a contaminated water supply, and inefficient systems of refuse and night soil collection, had led to a serious deterioration of living conditions. Furthermore, the fact that rows of shophouses were traditionally constructed back to back with those in the next street along, meant that entire city blocks were completely built over with no intermediate spaces in between — "huge agglomerated masses of bricks and mortar" was how the *Straits Times* described them in an editorial of 12 June 1888.

Incredibly, given the circumstances, there were only occasional and relatively minor outbreaks of cholera, smallpox and bubonic plague, but the threat of a wholesale epidemic was ever present, compelling the authorities to act. Studies were commissioned and reports compiled, which eventually culminated in the introduction of new building regulations and Ordinances in 1907.

An important innovation was the introduction of a backlanes scheme, the idea here being to open up a corridor between the densely packed terraces of back-to-back shophouses, thereby bringing to their occupants "the blessings of light and air". Backlanes would also facilitate the collection of night soil — which could now be taken out through the rear of the property rather than being carried all the way through the house to the front entrance — and also serve as a firebreak, fire being a constant hazard in the days of oil lamps and open-hearth cooking arrangements. Lastly, backlanes would help to prevent the spread of contagious diseases.

All in all, backlanes were deemed to be a very good thing, but they had a major impact on the development of the Singapore shophouse, ultimately leading to the adoption of a new layout — an L-shaped plan — which in a few years became the standard configuration for all new shophouses, thus bringing about the end of the skywell as an integral feature of shophouse architecture.

ABOVE   This photograph of a street in Chinatown in 1907 — the home of rickshaw coolies, it would seem — graphically illustrates the lamentable living conditions that prevailed there at that time. The problem was in part a legacy from the days of the East India Company when officialdom had taken a pretty *laissez-faire* approach to municipal matters, but 40 years after the transfer of Singapore to the jurisdiction of the Colonial Office, not that much had changed, except that the situation downtown had got a whole lot worse. Courtesy of NAS.

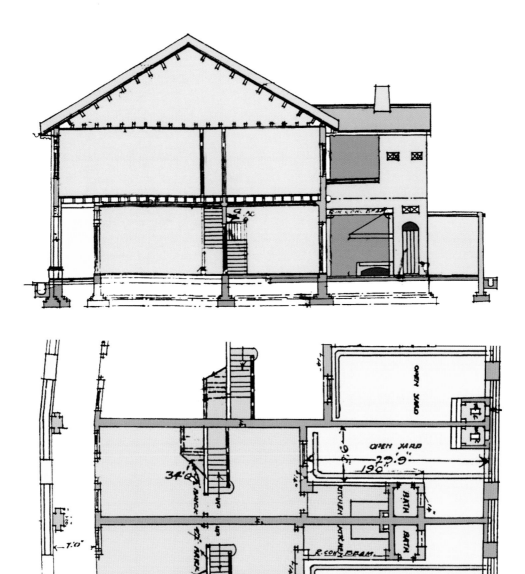

ABOVE New building regulations, introduced in 1907, required that one third of a property be left as "open space". Somewhat perversely, airwells were not deemed to constitute an open space and so, more often than not, they were dispensed with altogether, while the back of the property was divided equally between an open-air yard and a rear extension in order to comply with the one-third open space requirement. This led to a new L-shaped configuration for the shophouse and the traditional Chinese skywell became a thing of the past.

RIGHT View of a backlane running between Stanley Street, on the left, and Telok Ayer Street on the right; previously, the shophouses in these two streets would have stood back to back.

# THE ROCOCO SHOPHOUSE

The new building regulations introduced in 1907 seem to have resulted in a lull in shophouse construction, a situation that was exacerbated by economic woes, but by the eve of World War 1, the Singapore shophouse stood poised on the threshold of a new era, characterised by a revival of interest in surface ornamentation, a kind of "second coming" of the highly decorated shophouse, that put even the Baroque shophouses of the turn of the century in the shade.

As an ensemble, this riot of surface ornamentation was quite extraordinary. Searching around for a descriptive label for this new direction in shophouse architecture, images of wedding cakes come naturally to mind, but ultimately Rococo is probably the better term and one that is also historically more appropriate.

Rococo was a highly decorative style of 18th-century architecture that grew out of the preceding Baroque era. "Elegant and frothy" is how the *Oxford Dictionary of Architecture* describes it, "drawing on marine and shell motifs found in grottoes, and incorporating ogees and C-scrolls, asymmetrically disposed around frames [and] cartouches ... like a mixture of coral, seaweed, and stylized foliage." It continues: "Rococo designs included aspects of Chinoiserie, Gothick, and even, in its later phase, Hindoo decorations." In addition, "Rococo designs included bandwork, diaper patterns, espagnolettes, scallop-shells and scroll-work, incorporated in schemes of unsurpassed grace and beauty." Unsurpassed grace and beauty might be going a little too far, but otherwise that more or less fits the bill, so Rococo it is.

Some of the best surviving streets of Rococo shophouse architecture are to be found in Little India, in particular on Desker Road, which is all the more remarkable for largely being the work of one man, George d'Almeida. Entering the final stage of his career — d'Almeida died around 1920 — he led the way forward one more time with his new, Rococo-inspired style of shophouse architecture.

ABOVE One of the most striking landmarks on Jalan Besar are two, three-storey terraces of Rococo-style shophouses, symmetrically arranged on either side of the junction with Veerasamy Road. Richly endowed with leafy festoons and garlands and just about every other kind of floral motif in high relief, they epitomise the wedding cake aesthetic of the late 1920s and are among the best surviving examples of this exuberant style of architecture to be found in Singapore.

OPPOSITE TOP Detail of a richly ornamented shophouse in Syed Alwi Road, featuring Peranakan window tracery, swags, a band of egg-and-dart moulding, dentils, and an interesting reinterpretation of the Corinthian capital, with all the best bits highlighted in contrasting colours.

OPPOSITE BOTTOM Easily the most famous example of the Rococo style is this row of nine shophouses at Syed Alwi Road, whose enormous *œil-de-bœuf* (ox-eye) window openings would not look out of place on the attic floor of the Paris Opera.

D'Almeida started out in 1915 with a row of five shophouses on the south side of Desker Road, between Kampong Kapor Road and Jalan Besar, for a Mohamad bin Hadjee Omar Esq. This established the basic parameters of his new-look shophouse, which he then proceeded to apply to the north side of the road in a series of four separate commissions comprising 14 units between 1916 and 1918. His client, as before, was Mohamad bin Hadjee Omar, but d'Almeida also designed a single shophouse in the same style on the opposite side of the road for Hadji Gulas Kahn Suratee in 1918. By the time d'Almeida was through with Desker Road, Rococo was firmly established as the leading shophouse style for the immediate post-war period.

TOP ROW  A beautifully restored Rococo shophouse in Syed Alwi Road (left); Rococo apartments at Bukit Pasoh, from 1926 (middle); unusual rusticated secondary pilasters in Desker Road (right).

BOTTOM ROW  George d'Almeida's extraordinary World War 1 Rococo development at Desker Road, the architectural equivalent J S Bach's *Goldberg Variations*.

高氏公會

錢山宮汕頭邑同鄉會
Qianshangong Shantoucun Association

# 1920s CHINOISERIE

Coincident and no doubt in part contingent with the appearance of the Rococo shophouse one finds a revival of interest in traditional Chinese decorative elements taking their place alongside ornamentation of a more European provenance. The idea itself is perfectly in keeping with the Rococo style — Chinoiserie was like the Orientalist arm of the Rococo movement back in 18th-century Europe — but the execution is wholly Singaporean.

These Chinese decorative elements include dragons, phoenixes and the 12 animals of the Chinese zodiac, all of which were chosen as much for their iconographic import as for their decorative potential. Images of flowers and birds are also common, again each with its own auspicious significance. Vases with peonies, symbolising wealth, honour and tranquillity, are a recurrent motif, as are images of cranes, which symbolise longevity — the Chinese believe that these birds live to a very great age. Tigers also symbolise longevity, but more importantly they exert a powerful protective influence, the word for tiger (*hu*) being pronounced the same way as the word "protect". And then there is the ubiquitous bat which is a visual pun for prosperity and well being, the term for bat, *fu*, being a homonym of the word for good fortune and happiness in Chinese; not surprisingly bats are to be found just about everywhere.

These ideas and representations are all part of the traditional Chinese repertoire, but they seem to have fallen into abeyance with the rise in popularity of Classical forms of ornamentation and decorative motifs. In the 1920s, however, there was a renewed enthusiasm for this kind of thing. This time around, though, the images have a more rounded, sculptural quality — particularly the animals — whereas previously they had been depicted more in relief.

Sam Leong Road, off Jalan Besar, is especially noteworthy for a remarkable terrace of richly ornamented townhouses from the 1920s which are liberally plastered with a profusion of auspicious animal motifs, including prosperity bats, propitious peacocks, protective tigers, long-living cranes and mischievous monkeys.

LEFT Similar displays of Chinese bestiary can also be seen on Kitchener Road, which is the next street up from Sam Leong, and again in Jalan Besar, on the opposite side of the road, just before the junction with Foch Road.

LEFT BOTTOM AND OPPOSITE BOTTOM One charming addition to the repertoire of traditional Chinese images are scenes of everyday life in the Straits Settlements — images of rickshaws and bicyclists, people playing football or walking the dog, and so on. Unlike the bats and peonies, or the traditional vignettes borrowed from Chinese temple architecture, these images have no particular symbolic significance or morally uplifting message. They are there simply to entertain and amuse.

OPPOSITE TOP One exception to this, is the inclusion of images of Sikh guards armed with rifles. They are placed on the façade to protect the building from robbers and other persons of ill-will who might harm its occupants; Sikhs were identified in the popular imagination as men of honour and integrity and during the colonial era were invariably employed in Singapore as guards outside banks, jewellery stores and pawn shops.

# EAST COAST SUBURBS

The Rococo style remained in vogue until the end of the 1920s, at which point in time it began to be overtaken by more Modern influences. One place, however, where one finds Rococo-style shophouses continuing to be built well into the 1930s is on the East Coast, where the terraces of middle-class housing in the Joo Jiat area, for example, clearly share a common ancestry with the shophouses at the far end of Little India.

The early development of Katong was as a kind of seaside resort, with holiday homes and beachfront bungalows nestling among the coconut groves. In time, however, the area back from the sea became increasingly built up with terraces of shophouses and townhouses. Katong's heyday was between the wars, where it was seen as a respectable upper middle class neighbourhood, something that is reflected in the quality of the surviving shophouse and townhouse architecture from that period. For the most part the style is a little quieter that the full-on Rococo found in Little India, but there are still some spectacular flights of fancy in some of the surface ornamentation.

The enclave of streets laid out between Joo Chiat Road and Still Road contain many fine examples of late-1920s and 1930s terrace houses in a range of contemporary styles: neo-Classical, Peranakan and Chinoiserie. Two of the finest streets in the neighbourhood are Koon Seng Road (right and opposite top left) and Everitt Road (opposite top right) where the style is Rococo with a dash of Chinoiserie. There is a Teochew saying that goes "*gim Tanglin, ngeng Katong*", "golden Tanglin, silver Katong", which perfectly reflects the relative desirability of these two upmarket residential areas. For middle-class Peranakans between the wars, Tanglin, with its black and white bungalows and *towkay* mansions, may have been a little beyond their reach, but Katong with its (then) close proximity to the sea was a very attractive alternative.

OPPOSITE TOP  This row of townhouses in Everitt Road is distinguished by lively Chinoiserie panels beneath the first floor windows, which depict all manner of weird and wonderful beasts — some real, some imaginary, and some, halfway in between.

OPPOSITE BOTTOM LEFT  Rococo corner block at the junction of Joo Chiat and Koon Seng roads, from 1928; most of the shophouses along Joo Chiat Road were built around this time.

OPPOSITE BOTTOM RIGHT  The URA award-winning, Sandalwood Terrace, was recently converted to condominium-style townhouses by SCDA Architects. Clever manipulation of sightlines from the street conceal the presence of a five-storey apartment block at the rear of the terrace.

RIGHT  Accommodating Singapore's burgeoning middle class was a major problem during the interwar years and single-storey terrace dwellings, generically referred to as "barrack houses", provided a cheaper alternative to the two-storey shophouse. This nicely-detailed terrace on East Coast Road, where the main living floor is raised a little off the ground in the manner of an Anglo-Malay bungalow, is typical of the style.

# BLAIR PLAIN

Westward expansion of the town in the interwar years was con-strained by largely physical factors. Unlike the East Coast, which was flat, there were hills to the west of town and Keppel Harbour and the port facilities at Tanjong Pagar prevented further growth along the coastline. There was, however, one small area that lent itself to residential development and that was the neighbourhood known today as Blair Plain — Spottiswoode Park, Everton Road and the eponymous Blair Road (Blair was a ship's caption who built himself a house overlooking the harbour at Spottiswoode Park in 1895).

Wee Teck Moh was responsible for some of the early Everton and Spottiswoode houses that were erected before World War I, but most of the houses on Blair Plain date from the early 1920s. Together they constitute some fine examples of the more refined Rococo townhouse style, a kind of west-end counterpart to the residential terraces that were being built on Singapore's East Coast at around the same time.

ABOVE Some of the earlier houses on Blair Road might seem a little amateur in terms of their detailing — the architect who designed this stretch has yet to be identified — but they have a certain whimsical charm nonetheless.

OPPOSITE Many of the houses along Blair Road were designed by leading British architectural practice, Swan & Maclaren. This corner site, comprising six units, was commissioned by Messrs Seow Poh Leng and Seow Chee in 1921.

ABOVE  A pair of very fine, Baroque townhouses on Spottiswoode Park Road, with paired eagles mounted on either side of the entrance to the forecourt. In Chinese iconography, the eagle (or hawk) is a symbol of courage, which might provide a clue to their former occupants.

OPPOSITE TOP  A row of late 1920s townhouse, Blair Road, recently painted in pastel tones.

OPPOSITE BOTTOM LEFT  End of terrace sites often provided the opportunity for something a little more adventurous as we see in this townhouse on Blair Road. Somewhat wider than the usual shophouse, it is set back from the street and has a first-floor loggia that turns the corner.

OPPOSITE BOTTOM RIGHT  Colourful front porch of a townhouse, Spottiswoode Park Road.

# NEO-CLASSICAL TOWNHOUSES

The Neo-Classical townhouse appeared on the scene around the same time as Rococo, but was almost its direct opposite, the excessive use of ornamentation and decorative flourishes being rejected here in favour of a quieter, purer form of Classical architecture, deployed with a minimum of fuss.

No doubt economy had a part to play in the rarefaction of these shophouse facades, but there was a bit more to this pared-down Classicism than simple parsimony. In the aftermath of World War I, the *fin de siècle* exuberance of the turn of the century may have seemed a little out of place resulting in a desire for a more restrained approach. At the same time, it was also part of a more general Neo-Classical revival in Western architecture.

ABOVE  The first shophouses on Kreta Ayer Road were erected during World War I and marked the last phase in the westward expansion of Chinatown. The townhouses depicted here date from the 1920s and reflect a remarkable shift in architectural tastes between pre- and post-war eras. The pre-war period was dominated by the Baroque townhouse, but after the war there was a marked preference for a less ostentatious neo-Classical style of architecture.

RIGHT  Emerald Hill *pintu pagar*, with a decorative motif not unlike a Grecian urn.

OPPOSITE BOTTOM  A terrace of 10 neo-Classical townhouses at Emerald hill, designed by the Tamil architect, R T Rajoo, for Towkay Low Koon Yee in 1924. Despite a prolific output — he designed some 20 townhouses on Emerald Hill, and another 10 around the corner in Saunders Road, as well as a large number of bungalows, shophouses and various other types of building — almost nothing is known about Rajoo, save to say that he was a prominent member of the Tamil community and that he died at his house in Tank Road on the morning of 24 October 1928.

1 9 2 8

ABOVE The leading shophouse architect of
the interwar years was without doubt Josiah
Bartholomew Westerhout. Westerhout started
out as an apprentice draughtsman with the PWD
in Malacca and first came to prominence in an
extremely successful partnership with Alfred
Lermit at the turn of the last century (see page
118). He was subsequently on his own for a
number of years, but in 1923 entered into a new
partnership with Scotsman William Campbell
Oman, who up until that time had been in the
employ of the colonial government. One of the
best surviving examples of their work is this
superb row of townhouses at Bukit Pasoh, which
date from 1926 — a kind of late-Edwardian
Baroque with nicely turned Doric columns and
alternating bands of stuccoed panels and fair-
faced brickwork.

# SHANGHAI STYLE

The 1920s was a time of alternating periods of boom and bust, which eventually culminated in the Great Depression of 1929. During this period, Singapore continued to grow both in terms of its participation and integration in the global economy, as well as physically in terms of population and the expansion of the city. New building technologies such as steel-frame construction techniques, reinforced concrete and improved lift design, paved the way for Singapore's first high-rise skyline, turning the waterfront into a modest approximation of Shanghai's famous Bund. Landmark buildings during this period include the Hongkong & Shanghai Bank (1921), the Ocean Building (1921–23) and the Union Building (1922), all designed by Swan & Maclaren on Collyer Quay.

As at other times, local architects and builders were influenced to a certain extent by contemporary public and corporate buildings that were going up around them, buildings designed by professionally trained British engineers and architects either in private practice or else in the employment of the colonial government. If you were a successful *towkay*, you too wanted your business premises to look a little like the blockbusters down on the waterfront, even if it was only a three-storey shophouse that you were operating out of.

LEFT  Four-storey lodging house at the corner of Ann Siang and Erskine roads, designed by Westerhout & Oman in 1924. The building, which comprises a kind of pared-down Classicism, augmented by Art Deco flourishes, would not have looked out of place on the Shanghai Bund one feels.

OPPOSITE  Shanghai Deco in Kandahar Street (top) and Bukit Pasoh (bottom).

# THE MODERN ERA

The first modern influences in shophouse architecture began to make themselves felt in the early 1920s. By this time, rapid advances in transport and communications, meant that Singapore was much more in touch with what was happening in other parts of the world and this included developments in architecture as much as anything else. People had seen Manhattan's skyscrapers in the movies and read about the glass-box style of the German Bauhaus school and the white cubes of Le Corbusier's "Purist" architecture in the press. They wanted their own buildings to be a part of this brave new world and that included shophouses too.

As far as the Singapore shophouse is concerned the advance towards Modernity proceeded through four stages. The first took the basic Classically-influenced archetype and pared back the detailing even further; "Stripped Classical" is the term that this style of architecture usually goes by. The second phase in modernising the shophouse went one step further and removed the detailing altogether. Economy was no doubt one reason for this, but there is also a discernible design ethos to this utterly pragmatic or utilitarian approach; this was not just doing things on the cheap, but reflected a functionalist or rationalist approach to design. The third was wholly Art Deco in inspiration. Late Deco that is — what is usually described as "streamlined Moderne", with the emphasis on curved corners, strong horizontal lines and protruding sun visors, "eyebrows" as they are sometimes referred to. Lastly, there was out and out Modernism à la the Bauhaus school of architecture, represented by Walter Gropius and Mies van der Rohe — flat roofs, sheer façades and steel-framed windows.

ABOVE Slobodov Petrovitch's starburst façade for Malayan Motors Showroom on Orchard Road from 1925 (the right-hand building in this photograph) is one of the few examples of the more decorative end of the Art Deco spectrum extant in Singapore.

OPPOSITE TOP RIGHT Shophouses at the junction of Keong Saik and Teck Lim Road, Bukit Pasoh, designed by Kwan Yow Luen for Messrs Ng Eng Kee & Lee Kum Seng in 1938. Remarkably, Yow Luen was completely self-taught and never worked for anyone else but himself; he started out in the late 1920s designing Rococo-style shophouses, but a decade later had progressed to streamlined Moderne.

**BELOW AND BOTTOM LEFT** Stepped parapets and flagstaffs were characteristic features of Singapore's tropical Deco era. No building could properly consider itself modern unless it had a flag flying from the top of it, it would seem!

**BOTTOM RIGHT** Tropical Deco continued to be popular in Singapore long after its "sell-by" date elsewhere. The Singapore Metal and Machinery Association in Jalan Kubor dates from the 1960s.

# A NEW PROFESSIONALISM

Generally speaking, it was the first postwar generation of European architects who were the early pioneers of the Modernist movement

in Singapore. They included Public Works Department Architect, Frank Dorrington Ward, who designed the Kallang Airport buildings; former Government architects J M Jackson and E V Miller; the multi-faceted Frank Brewer who would later be responsible for the Cathay Building; Swan & Maclaren partner, Frank Lundon, and his colleague, British-trained Serbian architect, Doucham Slobodov Petrovitch who designed the Federated Malay States Railways terminus at Tanjong Pagar; Swiss engineer, H R Arbenz, and Frenchman, Emile Brizay, also an engineer, who was responsible for the recently restored Ford Factory on Bukit Timah.

With the exception of J M Jackson and Frank Lundon, these were all professionally qualified men with degrees and diplomas from schools of architecture and engineering. Again aside from Jackson who joined the Municipality in 1912, they all came to Singapore after World War I and would have been familiar with the latest developments in the realms of both architecture and engineering in Europe at that time: primarily the Bauhaus and De Stijl movements. It was only natural then that they should be the pioneers of Modern architecture in Singapore.

When it came to shophouses, though, the leading Modernists were primarily local men. There was, however, a difference to previous generations in that during the interwar years we see the advent of the first professionally qualified Singaporean architects, E C Seah, who obtained a BSc in engineering from Armstrong College, Newcastle-Upon-Tyne, in 1910, being an early instance of this. For most Singaporeans, though, overseas study was simply not an option. A major step forward in the direction of a new professionalism came in 1923 with the establishment of a Singapore Society of Architects, followed by the passing of an Architects' Ordinance three years later. The latter legislation required practicing architects in the Straits Settlements to be either a Fellow, Associate or Licentiate of the Royal Institute of British Architects, or else a member of the Society of Architects. Alternatively, they should be in possession of a diploma in architecture from a recognised

RIGHT Four-storey apartment block on the corner of Tanjong Pagar and Kee Seng Roads, designed by H R Arbenz, for Messrs Credit Foncier d'Extreme Orient in 1937. Arbenz came from an engineering background with a BSc from the Eidegnossisches Polytechnikum, Zürich.

BELOW Maybe the climate had something to do with it, but Singapore's tropical Deco architecture, bears a remarkable resemblance to the architecture of Old Miami Beach. More likely, though, it was an increased exposure to contemporary architectural advances via architectural journals and glossy magazines, which were now more readily available in an era of rapidly improving communications. The cinema, too, had a major impact, introducing Singaporeans to the architecture of the major world metropolises — London, Paris, New York, and, closer to home, Shanghai.

educational establishment in the UK or a British territory. The last point was an important one because it meant that aspiring local architects could now sit for the qualifying exams in Singapore without having to study overseas.

Interestingly, most of these candidates opted for a qualification in engineering rather than architecture *per se*, and it was perhaps their familiarity with the latest developments in construction techniques and building technologies, most notably the use of reinforced concrete, that attracted them to Modernism.

# TROPICAL DECO

Art Deco is a slippery fish to define; the term only gained currency in the late 1960s and therefore from the outset was always applied

ABOVE  One commonly finds later Deco buildings inserted amongst the older building of Chinatown, pride of place in this instance going to W T Foo's four-storey masterpiece for the Dried Foods Guild in 1940.

OPPOSITE TOP  The upper end of South Bridge Road was rebuilt from the 1930s through to the end of the 1960s. The style of architecture is predominantly tropical Deco with an occasional nod in the direction of Bauhaus.

OPPOSITE MIDDLE LEFT  Five shophouses in Teo Hong Road, from 1938, with hugely extended *brise soleil*.

OPPOSITE MIDDLE RIGHT  A trio of tropical Deco-style shophouses on Club Street dating from 1927 and 1938.

OPPOSITE BOTTOM LEFT  Yong Nan Hotel, Geylang, designed by Chan Tong Yew in 1940 in streamlined Moderne style.

OPPOSITE BOTTOM RIGHT  Apartments in Madras Street, designed by the Singapore Improvement Trust, forerunner of today's Housing Development Board, in 1940. The Trust, or SIT as it was popularly known, was established in 1926 to help alleviate the appalling living conditions of Singapore's urban poor.

retrospectively. At the time that they were being built, the buildings that today are commonly identified as being Art Deco in style, would simply have been described as "modern", period.

Excoriated by both Classicists and Modernists alike for its frivolous and indiscriminate use of ornamentation, Art Deco architecture nevertheless owes something to both these schools. On the one hand, it took the formal properties of Classicism and modernised them — simplifying, essentialising, even caricaturing the various decorative elements, to give us the "stripped Classical" look mentioned earlier. At the other end of the spectrum, it took the cubist geometry of the Modernists and jazzed it up a bit, adding decorative zig-zags, sunburst cartouches and a range of ethnographic motifs drawn from ancient Egypt, Mesopotamia, China and Japan, even native American traditions. As Art Deco authority, Tim Benton, comments: "Most Art Deco buildings can be attributed to these two categories 'Modernized Classicism' and 'decorative Modernism'." Somewhere in between, though, we get a style called streamlined Moderne, which drew its inspiration from an almost millenarian belief in the redemptive qualities of science and technology, manifest as a fascination with fast cars, aviation, wireless telegraphy and domestic gadgetry — vacuum cleaners, coffee-making machines and the like. This was a style that emphasised curving, streamlined forms, strong horizontal lines and quasi-nautical elements, such as railings and porthole windows — the French passenger liner, SS *Normandie*, was an iconic inspiration, hence the term *moderne*.

Streamlined Moderne reached its height in the late 1930s and was especially popular in Singapore where adaptive responses to the local climate gave rise to an alternative description of the style as tropical Deco. As far as the Singapore shophouse is concerned, tropical Deco makes its first appearance in the early 1930s, but enjoyed an enduring popularity that survived well into the postwar era; in this respect, it represents the last major stylistic innovation in the shophouse tradition.

# HO KWONG YEW,
## MODERN MASTER

Ho Kwong Yew was easily the most talented of the Singaporean architects who took up Modernism in the years leading up to the war

in the Pacific. Born in 1903, the son of a tailor, Ho entered the PWD in 1922 as an apprentice under Government Architect H A Stallwood before transferring to the Municipality as a draughtsman, where he worked on the plans for City Hall under Samuel D Meadows. In 1926, Ho left the Government to join forces with leading local Modernists Chung and Wong; the following year he sat for and passed the first qualifying examination of the newly constituted Board of Architects.

Ho remained with Chung & Wong until 1933 when he went out on his own, quickly establishing himself as a frontrunner in the Modernist movement in Singapore — his shophouses could be characterized as "tropical Bauhaus".

His architectural talents aside, Ho Kwong Yew was an enthusiastic supporter of the arts and vice-president of the Society of Chinese Artists, so regularly welcomed visiting Mainland Chinese artists to his house at Yan Kit Road. In the late 1930s, many well-known Chinese artists came to Singapore to sell their work in order to be able to donate the proceeds to supporting the war effort against the Japanese back in China and it was Ho Kwong Yew's association with these prominent anti-Japanese figures that eventually led to his tragic downfall. When the Japanese occupied Singapore in February 1942 they immediately set about eliminating all those who they perceived as a potential threat; Ho Kwong Yew was among the many thousands of Chinese who were rounded up and summarily executed in the early days of the Occupation.

LEFT Four-storey office block in Amoy Street for the Thye Ann Investment Co, from 1939. Stark and uncompromising in its Modernist fundamentalism, this was the shape of things to come on the eve of World War II.

OPPOSITE Ho Kwong Yew's 1938 Expressionist masterpiece at the junction of Circular Road and Lorong Telok — the shophouse as aspiring skyscraper.

# POST-WAR POSTSCRIPT

The tropical Deco shophouse was revived in the immediate postwar era and continued to be built right through the 1950s and even as late as the 1960s. In time, streamlined Moderne gave way to more functional box-like structures, typically with a cantilevered upper storey project over the five-foot way rather than being supported on piers to create an arcaded walkway. By the 1970s, though, the shophouse was on the way out, at least in the middle of town, where entire streets of shophouses were demolished to make way for huge new corporate-style office blocks and air-conditioned shopping malls.

However, with the advent of the 1980s, a more sympathetic attitude towards the conservation of old buildings gradually began to emerge. This culminated in the Urban Redevelopment Authority's Conservation Master Plan of 1989, whereby large chunks of Chinatown and other venerable neighbourhoods were gazetted as Historic Districts and Conservation Areas.

Since then, various conservation schemes and promotional campaigns have breathed new life into these historic areas — and we have seen not only a renaissance of the shophouse, but also its reinvention in a variety of new and unconventional guises: stylish business premises, sought-after residences, boutique hotels and on-trend bars and restaurants. Even though the shophouse has come a long way from its roots in ancient China, its undeniable popularity is plangent testimony to its enduring success as a tropical urban archetype — one that works as well today as when it was first introduced to these shores close to two centuries ago.

LEFT Bugis Junction; Hylam Street looking towards Malay Street. A former red-light district and popular tourist spectacle in the early years of the 20th century, this once-notorious area is now celebrated for housing Singapore's first air-conditioned streets.

OPPOSITE The old and the new, with the towering glass and steel edifices of modern Singapore's Central Business District as a backdrop to Bidwell's Lai Chun Yuen Opera House from 1897; in its heyday, the latter was just about as famous as a place of pleasure and entertainment as today's nightclubs and casinos.

# THE
# SHOPHOUSE
# TODAY

3

# THE SHOPHOUSE AS TEMPLE

TOP Huge amounts of time and money were lavished on temple decoration. Such projects brought traditional craftsmen and artisans from China to Nanyang city ports.

ABOVE The Kuan Yin Temple on Keong Saik Road, though purpose-built as a temple, is actually laid out as a double-fronted shophouse and is sandwiched between shophouses on either side.

OPPOSITE BOTTOM The Fuk Tak Chi Temple on Telok Ayer Street was built in 1824, just five years after the founding of Singapore. The temple is dedicated to Tua Pek Kong, a peculiarly local Malayan and Singaporean deity, originally worshipped in Penang.

Arguably the most important defining feature of traditional Chinese architecture is the courtyard, which was once the starting point for just about any architectural enterprise in China, domestic or otherwise. Be it a palace or a temple, the home of a mandarin, a wealthy land owner or a prosperous merchant — all of them, you will find, have at their centre, a courtyard, or *thing yuan*. The bigger the place, or more important the building, the greater the number of courtyards — the Forbidden City in Beijing has courtyards without end — but everywhere the principle remains the same.

In the case of temples, the general layout of the compound is actually very like that of a courtyard house, with the most prestigious structure — the pavilion housing the altar dedicated to the principle deities — (ideally) situated on the northern side of the central courtyard, facing south, and the main entrance directly opposite. Indeed, there are several temples in Singapore which are indistinguishable from courtyard houses, for example the old Tau Pek Tong temple tucked away on Palmer Road, off Shenton Way. But while a temple might be like a courtyard house, conversely, and just as easily, a shophouse could be a temple! The homogeneous nature of Chinese architecture, revolving as it does around the courtyard, means that the basic layout of shophouses naturally lends itself to their conversion into a place of worship and there are many instances of this in Singapore, two of which are featured in the following pages. Often the circumstances were such that some wealthy and devout *towkay* would, upon his death, leave his home to some religious institution that he supported during his lifetime.

OPPOSITE TOP The magnificent Thian Hock Keng Temple on Telok Ayer Street is dedicated to the goddess Mazu, Empress of the Heavens and guardian of seafarers. At the time that it was built (1839–1842), the temple stood on the shores of Telok Ayer Bay (subsequently reclaimed from the sea in the 1870s) and this was where junks bringing immigrants from China would put their passengers ashore, whereupon the newly-arrived *sinkeh* would go directly to the temple and give thanks to Mazu for their safe passage.

# SEAH SONG HOUSE (NANYANG SACRED UNION)

The Nanyang Sacred Union on River Valley Road was formerly the home of Seah Song Seah, the third son of Seah Eu Chin, the original "Gambier King", who came to Singapore from China in 1823 and

ABOVE  Right-hand temple of the Nanyang Sacred Union, dedicated to Lao Tze.

OPPOSITE  Forecourt and main entrance to Seah Song Seah's former home.

was one of the first to plant gambier in a major way. Song Seah's three brothers were Seah Cheo Seah, Seah Liang Seah and Seah Peck Seah, all of whom were prominent members of the Chinese community in the latter part of the 19th century. They were educated men, well-versed in the traditions of their homeland — family founder Eu Chin was the son of a minor official in imperial China — and all of them purposely incorporated Chinese decorative elements in their houses; Eu Chin and the eldest son, Cheo Seah, both lived in traditional courtyard houses on the banks of the Singapore River.

The oldest part of the building is the central portion, which was designed in 1896 by Almeida & Kassim. This was a free standing structure, the plan being based on a traditional, two-storey southern Chinese townhouse with a central airwell and a pair of courtyards on either side — there are correspondences with Tan Yeok Nee's house on Clarke Quay and the Sian Teck Nunnery at Cuppage Terrace (see pages 160-163). The front façade, though, is given a typical Singaporean treatment with a five-foot way style entrance porch, despite the fact that the building is set well back from the road and has a forecourt. The decorative detailing, however, is authentically Mainland Chinese with a rich *chien nien* frieze over the canopy roof and traditional gable apexes, representing the fire element, which signifies energy and passion.

The two side wings were added in 1903 — they were designed by George d'Almeida, his partnership with Kassim having been dissolved the previous year — and various other additions have been made at different times, but some idea of the original structure can still be appreciated if one stands at the centre of the airwell in the oldest part of the house.

Some time after Song Ong Seah's death in the 1930s, the house was acquired by the Nanyang Sacred Union as a place to practice their religious rites. It was actually quite a common practice for the home of a notable member of the Chinese community to be consecrated as a temple after their death, the basic configuration of a shophouse ultimately being derived from the same template as a Chinese temple; the correspondence is especially close in the case of the Song Seah house since the airwell in the main building is centrally aligned. Today, Song Seah's former home is a temple dedicated to Confucius — the central portion — while the two side wings are dedicated to the Buddhist Goddess of Mercy, Kwan Yin, on the left and the philosopher-sage Lao Tze on the right.

TOP LEFT  looking from the courtyard of the original house towards the left-hand wing, added in 1903.

TOP RIGHT  Despite being set back from the road, the five-foot way verandah has been retained.

ABOVE LEFT  Temple bell used to punctuate transitions, or different stages, in ritual performances.

ABOVE RIGHT  Gable apex ornament on one of the side wings.

LEFT  The original front elevation of the Seah Song Seah house as it was originally designed by Almeida & Kassim in 1896, before the addition of the side wings.

OPPOSITE  The central skywell of Seah Ong Seah's original residence looking towards the altar dedicated to Confucius, but which in Song Seah's day would probably have been dedicated to his ancestors.

# SIAN TECK TNG
## VEGETARIAN CONVENT

Unlike the Nanyang Sacred Union, which started out as the private residence of Seah Song Seah (previous pages), the Sian Teck Tng Vegetarian Convent at the end of Cuppage Terrace was from the outset intended as a place of worship and a refuge for women. The convent was designed by Yeo Hock Siang in 1903/1904 and is laid out on a symmetrical axis with two centralised airwells, one behind the other. Like the Seah house, there are two side wings, again symmetrical in plan, each with their own internal courtyards; the basic configuration is that of a Guangdong (Canton) townhouse, though again like the Seah house, the front elevation is like that of a Singapore shophouse, with the five-foot way as verandah.

A wealthy Teochew family who lived next door donated the land for the convent and the building was paid for by privately donated funds. Actually, "convent" is something of a misnomer in that the women who live there are not vocational nuns in the strictest sense of the term, but rather women without families or homes — many of the first generation of inhabitants, were simply unwanted daughters who were deposited on the doorstep. Nevertheless, they do all worship the presiding deities at the Sian Teck Tng, chiefly Tien Chi Lao Mu, or Venerable Mother of the Limitless Heaven, a kind of universal goddess figure in the Taoist

LEFT With much of the original furniture still in place and in use, the Sian Teck Tng Convent conjures up a vision of a Singaporean way of life as lived in the early years of the last century.

OPPOSITE TOP Front elevation, with steps leading up to the shophouse-style front verandah. Originally the two side wings were flat-roofed, single-storey structures with a terrace on top.

OPPOSITE BOTTOM LEFT Front verandah and entrance to the right-hand wing.

OPPOSITE BOTTOM RIGHT Central skywell.

pantheon, and Kuan Yin, the Buddhist Goddess of Mercy. Like most Chinese religious institutions, the Sian Teck Tng Covent is fairly ecumenical in outlook, but is principally Taoist in orientation.

What is especially remarkable about this building is the extent to which the original features have been preserved, right down to the traditional-style hearth, or *dapur*, in the kitchen at the back (though charcoal has given way to gas) (see page 77). Though beautifully maintained, this is not a restored building, but one that has survived more or less intact for over 100 years and there is a deep-felt sense of continuity with the past.

OPPOSITE TOP Traditional, etched glass lantern over the entrance porch; the characters above the door proclaim the name of the convent — Sian Teck Ng.

OPPOSITE BOTTOM Side passageway leading to the main altar dedicated to Kuan Yin; the sign over the doorway reads: "Respect when you enter; bow when you leave".

ABOVE Room with ritual paraphernalia for divination by casting "moon blocks" or *beijiao*; the answers to questions asked of the deity are filed in the pigeonhole cabinet and are dispensed according to the way in which the *beijiao* — two crescent-shaped pieces of wood, a little bit larger than a segment of orange, flat on one side and rounded on the other — fall.

LEFT Airwell and dining area; the characters over the top of the wall cabinet invoke harmony, peace and tranquillity.

# THE SHOPHOUSE AS CLAN ASSOCIATION

Clan associations were an important institution in 19th century Singapore. They helped new arrivals from China who shared the same surname to find their feet and looked after the welfare of clan members in general. This could mean finding jobs or accommodation, dispensing welfare for the poor, sick or elderly, and adjudicating in disputes between clan members. Clan property typically included burial grounds and it was the responsibility of the clan association to arrange for the proper burial of clansmen who had died in Singapore without relatives to attend to this duty. In the past, the funeral procession of a deceased member would have included bearers carrying the banners and lanterns of the clan association; members who did not attend could be penalised.

The clan association featured on this page is that of the Hakka community, the first to be set up in Singapore in 1822. Established by migrants from five counties in Guangdong province, it was called Ying Fo Fui Kun, the *ying ho* section of the name translating loosely as a mutual obligation for peaceful coexistence. This reflects the fact that the Hakka were a minority among the Hokkien majority of immigrants; they realised to succeed they needed to band together and help each other. As such, the clan association helped members find jobs, built the Ying Sin school for Hakka children and organized festivals and religious celebrations.

LEFT AND OPPOSITE Ying Fo Fui Kun is located on the corner of Cross street and Telok Ayer and occupies the same site as the original clan headquarters back in 1822, though the building has been rebuilt several times. Today's edifice dates from 1881/1882 and is in the Guangdong style, augmented by a pair of massive Roman Doric columns rising through two storeys.

**TOP AND BOTTOM** The Kong Chow Wui Koon, established in 1840, is Singapore's oldest Cantonese clan association. It was originally located on Pearl Street, but moved to its present home in to New Bridge Road in 1924. The building, which was designed by Westerhout & Oman, is a rather grand Edwardian Baroque affair with rustication, an arcaded front and loggias for the upper storeys, though the latter have since been filled in. Kong Chow (Gang Zhou) is a region of the Pearl River delta in Guangdong province, and it is where one of the last great battles of the Southern Song dynasty was fought before China was unified under the Mongolian Yüan dynasty in 1279. In the wake of the collapse of the Song dynasty, secret resistance movements sprang up teaching martial arts with the aim of overthrowing the Mongolian conquerors. Though their ambitions were never fulfilled, the tradition of martial arts training is continued to this day at the Kong Chow Wui Koon, which is famous for its excellence in this department, as well as for a special lion dance peculiar to this community; the Kong Chow Wui Koon Martial Arts and Lion Dance troupe was officially formed in November 1939.

TOP AND BOTTOM  Kiu Leong Tong Mutual Help
Association, Cantonment Road.

MIDDLE  Li Si She Shut (Lee Clan Association)
at Ann Siang Hill was founded in the 1860s by
immigrants from three different counties in
Guangdong Province. The interior is a treasure-trove
of memorabilia and old photographs documenting
the lives of past members of the association.

# THE SHOPHOUSE AS COFFEESHOP

The coffeeshop, or *kopitiam*, is a truly Singapore institution, whose local name admirably reflects the island's multi-ethnic society, *kopi* being the Malay term for coffee, as borrowed from the English, and *tiam* being the Hokkien word for shop. Shophouse eateries have of course been around for as long as there have been shophouses, but the origins of the coffeeshop as we know it today, with its bathroom-tiled walls, seems to have come about in the early 1920s when we find a sudden rush of applications to the Municipality for planning permission for "additions and alterations for a licensed coffeeshop in accordance with the Health Officer's requirements", or words to that effect. This was in response to new building regulations introduced as part of the colonial authorities' clean up campaign, but subsequently, we find the emergence of the purpose-built coffeeshop as a distinct building type, typically occupying a corner site and open on two sides, with high ceilings and a generous floor space, sometimes with an additional restaurant area upstairs.

In the past, the premises would have been furnished with round, marble-topped tables of local manufacture, with imported bentwood chairs, but in the modern era these have gradually given way to foldable Formica-topped tables and plastic chairs.

The coffeeshop was quite a different animal to the traditional Chinese teahouse, which as often or not doubled as a brothel or at least a place for socialising with *sing-song* girls if 19th-century accounts of Singapore are anything to go by. The coffeeshop owner, then as now, typically ran the drinks stall, providing his customers with coffee, tea, soft drinks, beer and other beverages, as well as breakfast items like *kaya* toast (a local spread made from eggs, sugar and coconut milk, flavoured with pandan leaves), soft-boiled eggs and other snacks. Other stalls would then be leased on the same premises to independent stallholders specialising in their own particular line of local delicacies — typically *dim sum*, Hokkien *mee*, *char kway teow*, *mee rebus*, *nasi lemak* and *laksa*. A particularly commendable aspect of this arrangement is that traditional dishes from different ethnicities are usually available at the same coffeeshop so people from different ethnic backgrounds, can all eat together in the same place.

ABOVE  Coffeeshop interior with old-style marble-topped tables and bentwood chairs; sadly these have often given way to modern plastic counterparts.

OPPOSITE AND TOP 1930s-style, purpose-built corner coffeeshop at the junction of Tembeling Road and Joo Chiat Place.

OPPOSITE BOTTOM The traditional coffeeshop is as much a place for meeting friends and socialising as it for grabbing a bite to eat. Moreover, in the modern era, where high-rise living has greatly diminished Singapore's once-vigorous street life, the coffeeshope performs an important social function in fostering a sense of neighbourhood and community.

# JOO CHIAT TERRACE HOUSE

The interwar period saw the emergence of new residential suburbs along Singapore's East coast as first the tram and then subsequently motorised transport enabled residents to commute longer distances to jobs in the city. The Katong area was a predominantly Peranakan or Straits Chinese neighbourhood, representative of Singapore's emerging middle class at that time.

Most of the shophouses in Joo Chiat Road were erected between 1929 and 1930 and the Tan house, which is a classic two-storey Peranakan East Coast townhouse, is very typical of that period. What is especially remarkable, though, is that the house has been in the Tan family ever since it was built — it originally belonged to the great grandmother of the present owners, who came to Singapore from China after World War I.

Equally remarkable is the fact that the basic fabric of the house has been preserved more or less in mint condition with many of the original fixtures and fittings still in place, apart from obvious improvements to the plumbing and an upgrading of the kitchen facilities from a charcoal *dapur*, to modern cooking appliances.

The front room, with its original encaustic tile floor, is dominated by a large and impressive altar; dedicated to the household gods, it originally came from China with great grandmother Tan. The principal deity is Kuan Yin, the Chinese goddess of Mercy — and friends and family members of the present owners regularly meet at the house to worship here.

LEFT TOP  Offerings to the household deities.

LEFT MIDDLE AND BOTTOM  In the upstairs room, an altar dedicated to the family ancestors (below) sits opposite another small shrine.

OPPOSTE TOP  Front room altar, dedicated to *Kuan Yin*, with marble-backed rosewood furniture, symmetrically arranged on either side in the traditional manner.

OPPOSITE BOTTOM  Many of the original fixtures are still in place, including the frosted glass panels in the windows to prevent passers by from looking in, and the 1930s-style Chinese lampshades dangling from the ceiling.

# 149 NEIL ROAD

The upper part of Neil Road began to be developed in the last decade of the 19th century and reflects a general exodus of wealthy merchants from Chinatown to more salubrious areas in the surrounding hills. The area was generally identified as a Peranakan enclave and the row of houses between Everton Road and Spottiswoode Park, which includes the Baba House (see pages 98–101), represents some of the finest examples of Chinese-style *towkay* townhouses still standing. Many of them were designed by Almeida & Kassim, who were specialists in this department, and 149 Neil Road, which has recently been completely renovated and restored is a particularly good example of the style.

The architects responsible for the makeover are Diego Molina and Maria Arango, from the architectural practice Ong & Ong, and enormous care was taken to respect the house's historical integrity while remodelling the interior to suit modern living. A thorough photographic survey was made of the whole building before work began and experienced Chinese craftsmen were commissioned to help restore the beautiful stucco reliefs surrounding the skywell. All the timber doors and shutters, including the elaborately carved *pintu pagar* half-doors at the entrance, were taken back to the wood and then repainted, or in the case of the *pintu pagar* applied with gold leaf. At the same time, wherever possible, original fixtures and fittings such as locks, hooks and window bars were retained, all of which contribute to the authentic feel of the building.

From start to finish it took eight months to restore the property and adapt the house to a modern lifestyle.

LEFT The entrance gate evinces a mix of both Chinese and Malay influences, indicating that the original owners were Peranakan.

OPPOSITE The front façade, with its *chien nien* frieze and canopy roof, plus exquisitely carved *pintu pagar* half doors and scroll plaques over the windows, bears all the hallmarks of a wealthy *towkay*'s townhouse at the turn of the last century.

**ABOVE AND OPPOSITE BOTTOM RIGHT**
One of the most outstanding features of the house is this Italian-made, cast-iron spiral staircase in the master bedroom, leading to the attic floor above. The staircase was stripped back to the metal and painted a clean white, whilst the gold-plated newel post, which is cast as a shepherd boy in an attitude of prayer with a sheep at his feet — the Christian imagery of the good shepherd tending his flock comes to mind — was carefully burnished to restore it to its original glorious state.

**LEFT** The pond was steam-cleaned to remove a century of moss and algae and craftsmen called in to restore and repaint the stucco reliefs of the skywell. A modern retractable glass roof was then installed to provide protection from the elements during inclement weather.

**OPPOSITE** The main staircase and the spiral staircases which lead to attic floor in the rear portion of the house; carved saloon-style swing doors leading to the bedrooms.

# 41 EMERALD HILL

The townhouses at 39–43 Emerald Hill were built at the same time and comprised a single development. They were designed by Wan Mohamad Kassim in 1905, when he was head of the architectural department of a firm led by the surveyor George Fernandez. The style is classic Chinese Baroque with splendid period interiors, including Chinese screens and furnishings. The client was one Goh Kee Hoon and it seems likely that the three units, which are interconnected, were intended for members of his family (he had two sons).

The most singular feature of these houses is the so-called library of the central unit. This is situated at the back of the house, at first-floor level, and it has windows on three sides overlooking the airwell at the back of the house as well as those of its neighbours on either side. It stands alone as a kind of independent pavilion, reached by a bridge or causeway — there are airwells on either side — extending from the main body of the house. No doubt it made the perfect retreat from the family for a man of studious or scholarly inclinations.

The house was acquired in 1989 by Dr and Mrs M C Tong who spared no effort or expense in seeking to restore the building to its original condition, with the consequence that together with the Baba House on Neil Road, it is one of the best surviving examples of a *towkay*'s townhouse from the turn of the last century.

LEFT  Nos 39 and 41 Emerald Hill; the two houses on either side of the main residence (No 41) have Chinese-style roofed entrances.

OPPOSITE  The entrance to No 41, with a pathway of Victorian-style encaustic tiles leading up to an impressive *pintu pagar*.

ABOVE LEFT The *pintu pagar* is unusual in that each door leaf is hinged about its central axis and can be folded back on itself.

TOP Inside the entrance: the characters over the door read "dancing phoenix", an auspicious reference to the vitality of the women of the house.

ABOVE Even the door jambs are carved and gilded.

TOP  Windows with fanlights overlooking the principal skywell.

ABOVE AND TOP RIGHT  The Classical detailing of the house takes the acanthus-leaf capital of the Corinthian order as its starting point, but is not quite what your average Roman might have expected.

BOTTOM RIGHT  One of the airwells on either side of the bridge connecting the study to the main part of the house.

OPPOSITE TOP  The principal skywell with the lion-headed newel post of the main staircase in the foreground.

OPPOSITE BOTTOM  The most unusual feature of the house is the study, a bright, airy first-floor room with elegant Georgian fan-lit windows on three sides.

ABOVE  Because of unusual plan at No 41, with its broader-than-average width and four airwells, there are several inside-outside spaces and the whole house generally has a light and commodious feel to it.

# THE POET'S HOUSE,
## EMERALD HILL

The so-called Poet's House on Emerald Hill is the former home of Kuala Lumpur-born Dr Goh Poh Seng (1936–2010) who lived in

ABOVE  A door, with traditional *pintu pagar* acquired in Penang, leading to the back courtyard.

OPPOSITE TOP  The staircase was rebuilt and Dr Goh's collection of antique screens and panelling used for the windows overlooking the airwell.

OPPOSITE BOTTOM  A Victorian "Gothick" mirror and cabinet standing beside an apothecary's medicine chest, together with a salvaged Chinese screen and early-20th century ceiling light, establishes an eclectic Peranakan mixture of European and oriental fixtures and furnishings.

Singapore from the 1960s until 1986, during which time he was a very active patron of the arts, writing poetry and putting on plays and reviews, in between practicing medicine. His sometimes outspoken criticism of the establishment eventually led him into self-imposed exile in Canada, but prior to this Dr Goh had been one of the early pioneers in rehabilitating the shophouses on Emerald Hill.

Emerald Hill, with its elegant turn-of-the-century townhouses, was one of the first areas to receive attention when the Urban Redevelopment Authority of Singapore announced its plans for a massive urban conservation programme in August 1981. Dr Goh bought up one of the older houses in the street and commissioned architects William Lim Associates to restore and refurbish the property which was in a considerable state of disrepair at the time. Despite a sagging roof and other structural defects, it was decided to retain as much of the existing materials as possible in order to preserve not only the exterior, but also the internal character of the house. In addition, Goh had for some time been collecting antique timber panels and screens from a number of old houses, both in Singapore and Penang, where he had previously had a home, and it was the architect's brief to include these in the refurbishment of the building.

In the end, renovation work turned out to be much more extensive than originally envisaged, involving a complete removal of the entire roof as well as all the existing timber floor joists and floorboards. A jack roof and skylight were added over the newly-created internal courtyard and pool area, bringing light and air into the centre of the house, but the original roof tiles were reused, while the choice of materials used for renovation works, such as the *kapur* wood (*Dryobalanops* spp) floor boards were chosen because of their traditional associations. One exception was the white Carrara marble used for the principal rooms on the ground floor.

# JOHNSON TAN HOUSE

ABOVE Although the house was built at the end of the 1920s, the owner has enthusiastically set about giving it a turn-of-the-century makeover using authentic and original materials collected from ruined and dilapidated Chinese-style houses from elsewhere, including Malacca and Penang.

Mr Johnson Tan's house on River Valley Road was built in 1929–30 and is one of a pair of Westerhout-style townhouses with first-floor loggias, distinguished by a purpose-built garage at street level, an amenity made possible by the fact that the house is situated on the side of a hill; this added feature was apparently very prestigious.

The ninth child of a third generation Chinese family in Singapore, Mr Tan's passion is collecting antiquities relating to Chinese culture, many of them gleaned from his elder siblings. As well as restoring the house, he added older, more traditional features from an earlier period to this late '20s townhouse, including the front doors and *pintu pagar*, window shutters and interior screens. These he acquired over the years from old buildings that were either being demolished or gutted for modernisation.

Inside, Mr Tan has put together a veritable museum of Straits Chinese culture — altars and religious paraphernalia, furniture, paintings, ceramics, antique electrical appliances, including Deco-style pedestal fans and numerous valve wireless sets.

RIGHT  The townhouse is raised above street level with a terrace in front and a first-floor loggia (below) which is very typical of the period. Note the pre-cast concrete airbricks, set in the parapet wall, which superseded the green-glazed traditional Chinese version at around this time.

ABOVE The front room of Mr Tan's house with a shrine along the back wall dedicated to the household deity, Guan Yu; the altar is a family heirloom and was brought to Singapore from China. Guan Yu is the Chinese god of war but his presence in a domestic setting is to protect the house and its occupants from malevolent influences. On either side of the shrine a pair of couplet boards proclaim his virtues. One reads, "Loyal like the Sun and Moon," the idea here being that Guan Yu is as dependable as the alternation of these celestial bodies; while the other reads "As Patriotic as the Sky," in other words his patriotism has no limits. On the altar table in front of this shrine stand the figures of Xuan Shou (left) and Ma Ku (right), symbolising longevity, surrounded by porcelain fruit — the "Three Abundances" — peaches, pomegranate and Buddha's hand citron, again signifying a long and quite literally fruitful life, blessed with plenty of children.

LEFT AND OPPOSITE Entrance vestibule with Chinese console and mirror. The screen, which stands directly behind the front door, is placed to deter malignant agencies from entering the house, and was originally acquired from a house in Malacca; glazed windows were introduced into the houses of wealthy in the last decade of the 19th century.

OPPOSITE TOP This space was again originally the airwell, which has since been roofed over enabling the void to be turned into an upstairs sitting room. It is dominated by a huge mirror, made in Hong Kong, which was especially commissioned as a 70th-birthday gift for an important lady, presented to her by ten companies. It depicts Ma Ku presenting Xuan Shu with the elixir of longevity (see previous page), except that in this instance there is no Xuan Shu figure represented, the idea here being that Xuan Shu is the person standing in front of the mirror who sees their image reflected there and who thus becomes the recipient of this auspicious gift.

OPPOSITE BOTTOM The front room upstairs, with doors leading onto the loggia. Originally, this would have been the master bedroom, but today is used to house just a small portion of Mr Tan's huge ceramic collection, which interestingly includes many pieces salvaged from maritime wrecks.

TOP This room was originally the airwell, but has since been roofed over to create a family room and dining area, with a Chinese-style wall cabinet displaying Peranakan crockery and mother-of-pearl inlaid furniture. The black and white oil painting is based on a photograph taken of the Tan family when Johnson Tan was nine years old — he is the little boy in the middle; the colour painting is of his parents.

ABOVE Bedroom with a mother-of-pearl inlaid Peranakan bridal bed, originally acquired from Penang.

# CAIRNHILL TOWNHOUSE

This converted townhouse on Cairnhill was one of a row of ten originally designed by J B Westerhout in 1919 for the estate of the late Ong Sam Leong. Ong Sam Leong was one of Singapore's earliest speculative property and real estate developers, whose multifarious business interests included rubber planting, timber concessions and sawmills, as well as the Batam Brickworks; his sons went on to start the famous New World Cabaret and Amusement Park on Jalan Besar in 1923.

The conversion was carried out by Guz Wilkinson Architects, a private practice under the leadership of the eponymous Guz, which specialises in the design of tropical, eco-friendly buildings and homes. The client was a private developer who bought the house as an investment property; the architect's brief was that he should create a comfortable and spacious modern home, while retaining the character of the original building in relation to the front elevation and internal airwell.

To achieve this, the interior of the building was completely gutted and then rebuilt with a new three-storey extension, complete with rooftop swimming pool, at the rear. The footprint of the original airwell was retained, one of the concerns of the architect being to maximise the amount of natural light entering the core of the building. The floor of the airwell was then turned into an attractive water feature, to create a cool and tranquil interior space, enhanced by the quality of the light reflected off the surface of the water.

LEFT  The rear block, comprising a three-storey extension, is an entirely new addition to the shophouse. Seen here through floor-to-ceiling glass windows, it merges a modern aesthetic with traditional shophouse style.

ABOVE  The pool occupies the original skywell and is perfectly in keeping with traditional Chinese sensibilities where water and fish have positive connotations. Here, floating stepping-stones connect the front of the house with its rear extension. A glass roof directly above the stepping-stones affords protection from the rain while maximising the amount of light entering the innermost part of the building; the rest of the airwell is open to the sky.

LEFT  Looking front towards the back of the house; light-stained wood used for the doors, windows and furniture, enhances the client's desire for a "natural feeling" in the house.

# 55 SPOTTISWOODE PARK ROAD

The front elevation of 55 Spottiswoode Park Road is a classic example of Singapore Baroque, with keystones, Regency-style fanlights (at the first floor level), pedimented secondary pilasters and a Chinese-style canopy roof over the five-foot way verandah. One wonders, however, what the original owner — who may have been the so-called Pineapple King, Lim Nee Soon — would have made of the rooftop swimming pool at the rear of today's building!

Recently restored and modernised by the award-winning practice, Richard Ho Architects, this three-storey townhouse is itself the recipient of the Urban Redevelopment Authority's Architectural Heritage Award for 2010. Richard Ho was a natural choice of architect for the project, having engaged in a number of shophouse restorations in the past, including No 54 next door and just around the corner at Nos 25 and 26 Everton Road (see following pages). The design philosophy of the practice is that architecture should be "an expression of the continuity of the history of civilisation and the memory of cities", and we see this at work here where, despite a major rebuilding of the rear of the property, to accommodate the swimming pool on the roof, the ambience and historical references of the original building are still very much in evidence.

LEFT  The rear of the property was completely rebuilt to allow this third-storey, glass-sided rooftop swimming pool

OPPOSITE  55 Spottiswoode Park Road is the centrepiece in a trio of Baroque townhouses.

OPPOSITE TOP LEFT AND RIGHT  Although the staircase is new, the present owners, Louise and Edouard Merette, were keen to create an authentic feel for the house and the fretwork banisters are based on period originals.

OPPOSITE BOTTOM  Third floor bedroom with timber floors and jalousie-shuttered windows.

ABOVE  Master bedroom balcony with green-glaze Venetian balusters, behind which a Chinese-style lattice screen has been placed.

LEFT  Stucco reliefs and a pond with a statue of the Buddha occupy the airwell; a remote-controlled retractable skylight allows this to be covered over during inclement weather.

# 26 EVERTON ROAD

26 Everton Road was built as a pair, together with the house next door. The starting point in this radical makeover of the interior, again by Richard Ho Architects, was the airwell which had to be retained in accordance with the URA's guidelines for Blair Plain Conservation Zone. This was turned into the central feature of the house and, using the analogy of a lantern, enclosed with timber doors and windows, which let in natural light during the day, while concealed lighting in the niches set into the walls bathes the house with light at night.

Although in terms of the materials and detailing, the interior is starkly modern, every effort was made to ensure that the authentic spirit of a Chinese shophouse was maintained in terms of the spatial organisation of the house, both vertically and horizontally.

Completed in 1996, the house received an honourable mention in the 2000 Kenneth Brown Asia Pacific Architecture Design Award Program, where the jury commended the architects for maintaining "the integrity of its traditional urban context in a forthright and contemporary way."

LEFT The glazing bars of the central airwell echo the theme of a lantern allowing natural light to come streaming into the house at every level during the day.

OPPOSITE LEFT Staircase leading to the attic floor. The house is slightly atypical in that it is in effect two and a half storeys in elevation.

OPPOSITE TOP RIGHT Entrance with traditional *pintu pagar* half doors and "bat" vents over the windows.

OPPOSITE MIDDLE RIGHT Attic floor with half-height windows overlooking the street.

OPPOSITE MIDDLE BOTTOM The unobtrusive open-plan staircase, which reuses the original shophouse floorboards, allows light to filter through from the airwell to every corner of the house.

# BLAIR ROAD TOWNHOUSE

Blair Road was developed rather later that the other streets in the neighbourhood — Everton Road and Spottiswoode Park — and this is evident in the Rococo detailing which resembles contemporary terraces on the East Coast. This house and its neighbour were built in 1923 to a design by Swan & Maclaren who were responsible for most of the architecture in the street. Interestingly, they still have a central skywell, because this was a feature that was fast disappearing at this time. The latter was glazed over, however, even in the original, which has led the present occupiers to make an interesting patio space out of the rear courtyard, complete with a pond and a pergola.

The house has been sensitively restored without an extensive remodelling of the interior and retains many of the original features including stained-glass windowpanes and air vents.

**LEFT** Internal window overlooking the airwell, with original stained-glass panes.

**OPPOSITE** The rear courtyard features an ornamental pond with a colourful modern mural based on traditional Japanese woodcuts; a pergola turns the space into a shady retreat.

RIGHT  The front room upstairs has been turned into a sitting room with contemporary Asian artwork.

BELOW  Modern stained-glass doors and windows complement the originals and are in keeping with the 1920s aesthetic.

BOTTOM  The four-poster bed is a 250-year old antique brought over from China.

# BLAIR ROAD TOWNHOUSE (2)

This Rococo town house from the early 1920s was part of the original development of Blair Road as an upmarket residential neighbourhood, most of which took place between 1921 and 1923. The houses on this side of the street were designed by Swan & Maclaren, the leading architectural practice of the day, and they are all set back from the road, allowing for a forecourt in front. They are representative of the new L-shaped plan which replaced the traditional, "out of China" layout with a central skywell, though some of the other houses in the street still retain this feature.

Although evidently designed as upmarket townhouses for well-to-do families, as opposed to tenement dwellings, the original working drawings indicate that there was a kitchen on both the ground first floor. One might wonder why this was felt to be necessary, but as it happens the setup is very convenient for the present occupier: A florist, he uses the ground floor as premises for his business and retains the two upper storeys as a completely separate domestic space. This arrangement, of course, is very much in the traditional shophouse spirit.

LEFT  On the working drawings, the elevations are drawn without ornamentation other than the fluted pilasters, indicating that the Rococo detailing was left to the artisans responsible for its creation, no doubt in consultation with the client.

OPPOSITE TOP  The master bedroom overlooking the street is large enough to double as a private a sitting room.

OPPOSITE BOTTOM LEFT  The kitchen-cum-dining area is open to the elements and overlooks the airwell below.

OPPOSITE BOTTOM RIGHT  The original staircase is still in place, seen here leading from the first-floor sitting room to the attic floor above.

# THE SHOPHOUSE AS
# BOUTIQUE HOTEL

The ever-adaptable Singapore shophouse has been turned to a wide variety of uses in its time, ranging from biscuit factories to dental surgeries.

ABOVE A guest bedroom at the New Majestic Hotel retains the building's colourful windows and front balcony, but adds modern amenities — flat screen television, DVD player, retro-chic furniture and modern plumbing.

OPPOSITE TOP A collection of Loh's design classics from the 1950s, including a red Arne Jacobsen Egg chair (1959) and a Sella Bicycle Seat Stool by Achille Castiglioni (1957), graces the lobby of Hotel 1929. On the other side of the street, the shophouse façade of the Royal Peacock Hotel is clearly visible through floor-to-ceiling windows.

OPPOSITE BOTTOM The rooftop swimming pool of the New Majestic Hotel is decorated with a mosaic frieze on the wall and window portholes that allow swimmers to spy on those eating in the restaurant below.

A contemporary usage is as a boutique hotel, a characterful, low profile, though not necessarily low-budget, place to stay for the discerning traveller, who wants to soak up something of the local atmosphere at street level rather than opt for the bland international style of the major hotel chains.

There are several in the Bukit Pasoh area of Chinatown — the New Majestic, Royal Peacock Hotel, Hotel 1929, Chinatown Hotel, among them — and they combine comfortable modern hotel accommodation with an eclectic mix of Deco, Modern and Straits Chinese furniture, juxtaposed with contemporary Asian art works.

One of the pioneers of this movement of adaptive re-use in the hospitality industry is former lawyer turned hotelier Loh Lik Peng. With three small "hip hotels" in Singapore to date — Hotel 1929, the New Majestic and Wanderlust, all housed in former shophouse premises Loh says he is always aware of each particular area's history. "I don't want my hotels to stray too far from their local context," he says, "So I work closely with Singapore's National Heritage Board on renovations." This is evident in the fastidious façade renderings — but once you enter a Loh hotel, all resemblance to the traditional shophouse interior vanishes. 1950s Scandinavian chairs mix and mingle with antique prints, modern art and vintage lights; swimming pools on the roof and Jacuzzis on wood-decked terraces are other notable features.

The Club, one recently renovated boutique hotel on Ann Siang Road, also plays with the area's heritage in innovative ways. The area, comprising Ann Siang Road and Hill and nearby Club Street, was a remittance hub for early Chinese immigrants wanting to send money and letters home; it also housed a number of social clubs and clan association premises. As such, the designers have used this theme in the interiors. A number of friendly "messengers" in the form of individually hand-painted birds direct guests to the various facilities and calligraphy-style artworks adorn the guest bedrooms.

Design director, Colin Seah of Ministry of Design, explains his work: "In our spatial interpretations for The Club, we aimed to evoke a sense of accessible elegance and modern authenticity that connects the modern traveller with the heritage of the location without harping on the irrelevant past."

As such, the boutique hotel straddles the past and present admirably. Encapsulating the phrase "restoration for reuse", it maintains links with Singapore's past but looks to the future. And, with more openings each year, visitors can't get enough of them.

OPPOSITE TOP The lobby at the New Majestic Hotel, the interiors of which were conceived by Colin Seah of Ministry of Design, features exposed brickwork on the ceiling, a collection of iconic chairs and a dramatic Art Deco-style staircase that whisks guests to individually themed rooms and suites above.

OPPOSITE BOTTOM Each of the hotel's 30 idiosyncratic rooms and suites is different, but all have an ironic bent in their design, be it a blue leather barber's chair, a bed accessed by a stepladder or a stand alone Victorian bathtub in the middle of the room; each features modern Asian artworks.

RIGHT TOP A rooftop view of the Royal Peacock Hotel gives a bird's eye view of roof tiles and five-foot-way below.

RIGHT MIDDLE The Club in Ann Siang Road, recently opened by Harry's Hospitality, dates from 1927 and sports a pristine white façade with elegant Doric columns in the round and an expansive terrace on the roof. Inside, the interior décor pays homage to the area's *hui kuan* (clan associations).

RIGHT BOTTOM Hotel 1929 on Keong Saik Road, with its Shanghai-style stripped Classical façade, looks comfortably at home in a former (and present) red light neighbourhood, famous for its bars, girls and raffish street life.

# ACKNOWLEDGMENTS

The publishers wish to extend their special thanks to the people and organisations listed below for their assistance and guidance in the creation of this book. All books are a collaborative effort and this one in particular needed the help of a dedicated team of writer, photographer, editor and designer to bring it to fruition over the past four years. Also, we are indebted to the National Archives of Singapore for access and reproduction of images and building plans.

Even though most of the photographs in the book are by Luca Tettoni, we do feature a number of other images herein. Every effort has been made to contact and clear all such in this book, but some may have proven elusive or lost in the passage of time. The Publishers will be happy to correct any inadvertent use of any image not recognised in the picture credits and rectify any such omission in any subsequent edition or printing.

Geraldene Lowe-Ismael deserves a special mention for sharing her knowledge of all things Singaporean and contacts with us so generously. Many, many thanks. Marjorie Doggett who generously allowed us to use her photographs on pages 87 and 91; H. Lin Ho for photograph of Malacca interior on page 87; Ronni Pinsler for photo of Taoist symbol on page 30; Dr Erik Holmberg for advice on historical sources; Professor Ronald Knapp, who generously shared his encyclopaedic knowledge of Mainland Chinese architecture; Peter Lee for information relating to the Baba House; Johnson Tan for his help in translating Chinese characters and explaining various aspects of traditional Chinese iconography and symbolism; Jean Wee Mei-Yin, former curator of the NUS Peranakan House; Aaron Kao for all the line illustrations; Richard K F Ho of Richard Ho Architects; Guz Wilkinson of Guz Wilkinson Architects; Joanne Tan at Ong & Ong; Colin Seah of Ministry of Design; Emiko and Steve Golden; Loh Lik Peng of New Majestic Hotel and 1929; Dr Goh Poh Seng; Mr and Mrs M C Tong; Margaret Tan; Louise and Edouard Merette ; David Powe; BACS Pte Ltd; Blair and Elena Thomson; Residents of Sian Teck Tng Vegetarian Convent; Corinne Ferrari; Leslie Sodano; Peter Rose. Last but not least, a very big thank you to all the staff at the National Archives of Singapore, who have provided tremendous help and assistance in sourcing archival materials over many years.

# BIBLIOGRAPHY

Chen Congzhou, Pang Hongxuan & Lu Bingjie 2008 *Chinese Houses: a Pictorial Tour of China's Traditional Dwellings*. New York: Reader's Digest; Shanghai: Shanghai Press and Publishing Development Co.

Comber, Leon 2009 *Through the Bamboo Window: Chinese Life & Culture in 1950s Singapore and Malaya*. Singapore: Talisman Publishing Pte Ltd & Singapore Heritage Society.

Doggett, M .J. 1958 *Characters of Light*. Singapore: Times Books International (1985 reprint).

Heng Chye Kiang 2003 *'Traditional Houses in Chaosan,' in The House of Tan Yeok Nee: The Conservation of a National Monument*, pp. 20-39. Singapore: Winpeak Investment Pte. Ltd. and Wingem Investment Pte. Ltd.

Khoo Joo Ee 1996 *The Straits Chinese: A Cultural History*. Amsterdam/Kuala Lumpur: The Pepin Press.

Knapp, Ronald G. 1989 *China's Vernacular Architecture: House Form and Culture*. Honolulu: University of Hawaii Press.

— 2005 *The Chinese House: The Architectural Heritage of A Nation*. Singapore: Tuttle Publishing.

— 2010 *Chinese Houses of Southeast Asia*. Singapore: Tuttle Publishing.

Kohl, David G. 1984 *Chinese Architecture in the Straits Settlements & Western Malaya: Temples, Kongsis & Houses*. Heinemann Asia.

Lee Kip Lin 1988 *The Singapore House 1819–1942*. Singapore: Times Editions.

Lim, Jon 1993 *"The 'Shophouse Rafflesia': an outline of its Malaysian pedigree and its subsequent diffusion in Asia"*, Journal of the Malaysian Branch of the Royal Asiatic Society LXVI (1): 47-66.

Liu, Gretchen 1984 *Pastel Portraits: Singapore's Architectural Heritage*. Singapore: Singapore Coordinating Committee.

— 1996 *In Granite and Chunam*. Singapore. Landmark Books & The Preservation of Monuments Board.

Lip Mong Har, Evelyn 1991 *The Principal Architectural Characteristics of Chinese Buildings in Singapore*. Singapore University Press

Warren, James Francis 1993 *Ah Ku and Karayuki-san: Prostitution in Singapore, 1870-1940*. Oxford University Press (1993); Singapore University Press (2003).

Widodo, Johannes 2004 *The Boat and the City: Chinese Diaspora and the Architecture of Southeast Asian Coastal Cities*. Singapore: Marshall Cavendish.

Yeoh, Brenda 1996 *Contesting Space in Colonial Singapore: Power Relations and the Urban Built Environment*. Cambridge University Press (1996); Singapore University Press (2003).